# The Final Event

*Dawn of the Age of Truth*

## Robert E. Cox

# The Final Event

Robert E. Cox

© Robert E. Cox 2009

Published by 1stWorld Publishing
1100 North 4th St. Fairfield, Iowa 52556
tel: 641-209-5000 • fax: 641-209-3001
web: www.1stworldpublishing.com

First Edition

LCCN: 2008944212
SoftCover ISBN: 978-1-4218-9064-7
HardCover ISBN: 978-1-4218-9065-4
eBook ISBN: 978-1-4218-9066-1

Edited by Deborah Belle Forman

All rights reserved. No part of this book may be reproduced or utilized in any form or by any means, electronic or mechanical, including photocopying or recording, or by any information storage and retrieval system, without permission in writing from the author.

This material has been written and published solely for educational purposes. The author and the publisher shall have neither liability or responsibility to any person or entity with respect to any loss, damage or injury caused or alleged to be caused directly or indirectly by the information contained in this book.

# Acknowledgement

I would like to acknowledge my meditation teacher, the late Maharishi Mahesh Yogi, as well as my divine benefactors, who have shared their wisdom so freely with me and without whom none of my books would ever have been written. I would also like to thank Rodney Charles, my publisher and an old trekking friend, who made it possible for this book to be published in short order. Last but not least I would like to thank Deborah Belle Forman, my personal editor, for her inspirational role and tireless efforts to get this book ready for publication.

# TABLE OF CONTENTS

A Personal Preface . . . . . . . . . . . . . . . . . . . . . . . . . . . 9

1. The End Times . . . . . . . . . . . . . . . . . . . . . . . . . . . 19

2. Cycles Of Time . . . . . . . . . . . . . . . . . . . . . . . . . . . 33

3. The Ages Of Man . . . . . . . . . . . . . . . . . . . . . . . . . 47

4. Historical Evaluation . . . . . . . . . . . . . . . . . . . . . . . 69

5. Physical Survival . . . . . . . . . . . . . . . . . . . . . . . . . . 83

6. Spiritual Survival . . . . . . . . . . . . . . . . . . . . . . . . . . 93

7. A Vision Of The Coming Age . . . . . . . . . . . . . . . . . 119

   About The Author . . . . . . . . . . . . . . . . . . . . . . . . 131

# A PERSONAL PREFACE

In order for the reader to understand the basis of this work, some personal details will be useful. Almost forty years ago, at the age of nineteen, I made a decision to dedicate my life to the pursuit of spiritual enlightenment through the practice of meditation. At one stage I lived for nine years in a monastic setting, where I spent 8-12 hours in silent meditation every day, 360 days of the year, ate a pure diet, and practiced celibacy.

Over the years, my meditations resulted in a series of powerful cognitive visions, as well as visitations from various denizens of heaven, who literally descended from the sky. The first such visitation occurred was in 1972, when I was 20-years old and at home taking a summer break from my studies at Vanderbilt University.

That summer I decided to work for my father at his construction material yard, and I was staying in a small guesthouse on our family estate, which was separate from the main house.

Our family estate was located in the southeastern portion of the United States, and it was surrounded by deep forest, extending for miles. The woods were filled with large old growth trees—pine, magnolia, oak, and gum—with a lush carpet of vegetation growing beneath the leafy canopy. The tops of the trees often wafted in the breeze some 150 feet overhead and gave the impression that the forest was breathing and sighing, like some great and wondrous living being.

At the back of the property was a pond, surrounded by ferns, lilies and amarillos. There were several old cyprus trees, draped with strands of spanish moss, growing out of the placid water, whose shadowy depths swarmed with minnows, frogs, crayfish, bream, and large mouth bass.

Adjacent to the pond, over a wooded bank, was a beautiful spring-fed stream, with a sandy bottom over which danced playful currents of sparkling clear water, cold as ice. In those days you could drink directly from the stream without fear, and the water had a delightful sweet taste. This stream, about 20-feet wide, wound its way for miles through the forest, punctuated by sun-dappled white sandy beaches, dark swimming holes, hanging vines, and mysterious gnarled logs, the guardians of the stream.

The forest and river were everywhere teeming with life— butterflies, dragonflies, birds, squirrels, rabbits, raccoons, snakes, turtles, and darting fish. The forest resounded with the harmonious chirping of the birds, which echoed through the woods like the chimes of a temple, and small animals scurried through the undergrowth or leapt through the leafy branches of the trees. In the evening, the shadowy landscape would come alive with the chorus of crickets, cicadas, and frogs, which ebbed and waned like some orchestrated symphony, while fireflies danced in appreciation.

In the shade of a large oak and pecan tree, as well as towering long-leaf pines, and located halfway from the main house to the river stood the summer cottage, where I was staying.

I had only been meditating for about a year and a half, and it was around this time that I decided to lengthen my meditations. I would arise every morning about 4 am and meditate for two hours before leaving for work at 6 am. Then, upon returning home around 4 pm, I would meditate for another two hours before dinner. After my evening meditation, I would often take a walk down to the river that ran through the back of our property.

One late afternoon in early June, after finishing my meditation, I decided to stroll down to the river. The sun's rays slanted through the trees and danced upon the glistening leaves in the canopy.

As I passed through the gate leading to the river, I felt something click in my heart. Simultaneously, I felt an opening in the sky, as if the sky was but an extension of my heart. I stopped dead in my tracks, because I knew something very strange was happening.

Mt eyes and attention were naturally drawn to an enormous presence descending through the opening in the sky far above the trees across the river. Its conscious presence seemed to extend for miles around, to the very horizons of the curved earth, and it seemed to be heading directly toward me.

Although it was completely invisible to my physical eyes, I could sense this presence with my awareness as palpably as if I were seeing it, and I was astonished at its enormity.

When it reached the area in front of me, my hair stood on end, all of the breath left my lungs, and every cell in my body exploded with excruciating bliss. I spontaneously fell to the ground like a limp sack of wheat and buried my face in the sand. I was unable to gaze at the blazing spiritual glory before me.

I had no idea what was happening, but I knew without a doubt that the One I had always loved since the very beginning of time was all around me. I was literally blinded by love.

My heart turned into a burning block of ice, which sent cold electric bolts of divine ecstasy racing through my body and soul. Gasping for breath, I could do nothing but utter inarticulate cries of agonizing love and adoration, while my face streamed with tears, and my limbs trembled and shook. Like a worm on the earth, I could do nothing but grovel in the presence of such divine majesty—which was invisible to my physical eyes.

For the first few minutes, the floods of bliss that poured through my body and soul were both icy cold and burning hot simultaneously. The electric bolts racing out of my heart to every cell ripped open new channels of conscious life in my body, which had long been dormant or else non-existent, and this was excruciatingly painful. But at the same time, the experience was agonizingly blissful, because these were lightning bolts of divine love, which instantly healed my cauterized soul.

When I finally regained the ability to see and raised my head, I saw the conscious face of God all around me—in every grain of sand, in every blade of grass, in every piece of bark on the trees, in the sky up above. Everything I saw, wherever I looked, was blazing with the glory of God, which like an all-seeing Eye, filled with infinite compassion and love, gazed back upon me.

I raised myself to my knees and knelt there in absolute awe. I had no desire to breathe, nor did I need to. Every cell in my body was breathing in that Presence, and so my lungs had no need to move. For at least ten minutes, I sat there basking in that glory. My heart surged like an ocean and overflowed in tears that streamed down my face like running rivers.

Eventually, when I began to breathe again, a deep silence and indescribable peace, suffused with transcendent compassion, settled upon my soul. I was in a state of absolute oneness with Nature, and I saw everything around me as completely conscious and fully alive.

I was filled with boundless compassion, because I saw that though each thing was fully conscious and filled with the glory of God, the individual things did not know that this was so. I am talking about everything—each piece of bark on the surface of the trees, each blade of grass, each grain of sand. All were filled with the conscious glory of God, yet they themselves remained unknowing.

As a result, I spontaneously began to look upon all the things in Nature as my younger brothers and sisters, who were like souls dying of thirst in the midst of an ocean of nectar. While caressing the grains of sand, the blades of grass, the pieces of bark on the trees, I wept for them. I wept out of sheer compassion and love for the little things in Nature, which were like so many infants cradled in the arms of the Mother Nature—the Great Goddess, who was imbued with the face and presence of God. With an aching heart, I longed to liberate them, to open their eyes, to make them see the unbounded glory in which they were immersed, and which they ultimately were.

With the upsurge of this tender compassion, I felt Mother Nature smiling upon me. I felt Her embrace my soul like a child who had fallen astray and been brought back to suckle at her boundless Bosom. And then, with tears still streaming down my face, I started to laugh. I couldn't stop laughing because my joy knew no bounds—and all of Nature was laughing with me. We were laughing together as One.

After about thirty minutes the vision faded and my heart grew still. I wandered down to the river and when I gazed at my reflection in its surface, I saw that my eyes were as bloodshot as crushed beets. My shirt was drenched from my tears as well as the effusions from my running nose, so I took off my clothes and bathed in the river.

I washed my face, flushed my eyes, and let the cool waters soothe my aching body, which was raw from the power of so much emotion. As I let the waters flow over me, while the sun faded in the West, the sounds, sights, and smells of the forest enveloped my senses, and I felt at peace with Nature for the first time in years. My heart was overflowing with gratitude for I felt that I had finally come back home.

This was the first of several such visitations that took place over the years. As my awareness evolved and after I obtained gnosis, these visitations were used to impart knowledge to me, directly and intuitively, on the level of pure consciousness—with no words being spoken.

I was shown things that I scarcely understood at the time, and to deepen my understanding of these things I began to study ancient writings belonging to a broad range of traditions, including the Christian, Judaic, Hermetic, Vedic, and Egyptian.

Upon realizing that the Vedic literature was by far the largest of these ancient literatures, I undertook the study of Sanskrit so that I could plumb the hidden meanings of this remarkable body of wisdom, which, compared to the others, is relatively unknown in the West.

These studies, along with my own intuitive cognitions, afforded new insight into these ancient traditions of knowledge from around the world, and in many cases I discovered that the ancient sages and seers were talking about the very same things I had experienced and been shown by my benefactors. I realized then that: "The Truth is only One, though the wise may speak about it differently."[1]

Eventually it was made clear that these things had been shown to me for a reason. I was supposed to share the things I had been shown with the rest of humanity, in accordance with my own understanding and the language of the time.

This was a heavy burden for me, because I prefer solitude and seclusion, and am rather shy of public exposure. As a very private person, the thought of sharing such intimate revelations, weighed heavily upon my heart. Nevertheless, my instructions were clear, and so I started writing, every day, for hours at a time.

The purpose of these writings was to clarify in my own mind what I had been taught and shown, both through my own inner cognitions and through my divine benefactors. The problem is that much of the knowledge I received from these sources was cognized intuitively—without any involvement on the part of my mind or intellect.

In effect, I was given abstract seeds of knowledge, which had to be nourished and grown by watering them with deep and constant thought on the level of the mind and intellect, so that their branches, leaves, and fruit might evolve and come into my conscious awareness.

In this regard, I found that writing down my thoughts as they occurred made the abstract and multidimensional cognitions more concrete—more graspable to my mind and intellect. This process of growing trees of knowledge from their abstract seeds has occupied my time for the better part of thirty years.

In 1997 I published my first book, entitled *The Pillar of Celestial Fire: The Lost Science of the Ancient Seers Rediscovered*. This was my first stab at fulfilling my obligations by presenting an eclectic overview of a vast variety of subjects pertaining to the things I had been shown—in accordance with my understanding at the time.

After that publication, I thought and hoped that perhaps I was done. I thought that my public obligations were fulfilled, and that I could retire in solitude to continue my devotions and meditations, as well as my ongoing metallurgical research in alchemy, without any further distractions. Cutting off all communication with my friends, I retreated into my proverbial cave.

In actuality, I moved to Arizona to live in seclusion in a small trailer, parked in the high desert on the edge of the most uninhabited region of the continental United States. My friends were the rabbits and antelope that played outside my door. But I carried on with my writing, and my understanding continued to unfold—as if it were a never-ending process.

In time, I realized that I was not done—that several additional books would be required to fulfill my obligations, especially in light of my growing understanding. By this time the structure of knowledge growing within me had become quite developed, as if pictures first seen in hazy outline were becoming high-resolution laser images.

In May, 2008, Inner Traditions published my second book entitled: *Creating the Soul-Body: The Sacred Science of Immortality*. This was not my original title; I preferred "Stairway to the Sky: The Path of Immortality," because the book is not really about creating a soul-body but about the path of immortality.

This is the path by which enlightened souls, throughout the universe, since the beginning of time, have ascended the divine ladder, or stairway to the sky, rising up through all the starry heavens until they go beyond the boundaries of this physical universe and enter into the abode of immortality that lies deep in the bosom of the infinite.

I had been granted a preview of this cosmic journey by my divine benefactors years before, and this book was designed to present my understanding of what I had experienced in accordance with the teachings of the ancient Vedic, Egyptian, and Hebrew sages—who mapped out the same path thousands of years ago.

A third book is scheduled to be published in November of 2009 by Inner Traditions. Its current title is *The Elixir of Immortality: A Modern Day Alchemist's Quest for the Philosopher's Stone*. In this book, I present the fruit of my alchemical research, developed over the course of the last fifteen years, in simple, scientific language and in the context of much older alchemical traditions that once extended from China to Egypt.

Originally, my intention was to keep this alchemical knowledge to myself, for it reveals secrets that have never before been made public. In the past, the revelation of such secret knowledge was considered anathema—sure to bring about the curse of God. But in the summer of 2008, I received instructions from my inner benefactors that I was to publish everything I knew about the subject, without holding anything back.

My understanding is that the earth is about to undergo a major transformation, and that it was essential for this knowledge to get out into the public domain as quickly as possible, so that the elixir could be produced and made available to every human being on earth in times to come. So I quickly wrote the book and sent it off to my publishers.

In my early writings, I was loath to draw any attention to myself and wanted to remain invisible. Deliberately trying to hide my light under a bushel, I chose to embed my own intuitive insights within a more scholarly context.

In compliance with my inner guidance, from this time forward, I will adopt my own voice—the straightforward voice of one who has seen the truth, directly and intuitively, with the eye of the Self, and has tested and proved its veracity on the level of mind and intellect.

In times of old when a King sent a message to another King, a carrier pigeon might be employed to deliver the message. However, the pigeons were afforded no great honors. Upon delivering their messages they were merely set free—to fly back home.

That is how this small personality, identified with the mind and body writing this text, should be viewed. I am simply here to deliver a message from the King inside me to the King inside you. Upon delivering the messages entrusted to me, I hope that I, too, will be set free to return back home. Now that this preliminary personal revelation is out of the way, let us turn to the subject at hand.

# 1. THE END TIMES

## Apocalypse

The story presented in this book is as old as the hills. It is the story of the phoenix—the mythical bird that periodically immolates itself in the sacred fire, so that its mortal body is reduced to ashes. But out of those ashes a new immortal body is resurrected, much more glorious than before.

The myth of the phoenix is recorded in many ancient cultures from India to Egypt. However, it is as universally valid today as it was thousands of years ago, because it presents an archetypal description of spiritual transformation that is endemic to human consciousness. In fact, it is especially valid now, because we are about to witness the greatest such transformation that has ever occurred in recorded history.

Many of the ancient sages and seers foresaw this ultimate transformation through their powers of intuitive vision. They foretold that at the end of a long cycle of ages, spanning thousands of years, a huge transformation in human consciousness would take place.

All transformations in Nature involve a process of both destruction and creation. The old form of the seed is ripped open and destroyed in the process of creating the new form of the sprout. Similarly, in the coming global transformation the veil of ignorance, which supports old and false ways of thinking, will be destroyed, so that the light of knowledge, which supports new and more truthful ways of thinking, might shine forth.

The Greek term "Apocalypse" literally means "lifting the veil." The veil that is about to be lifted is the dark veil of ignorance that has largely covered the human soul for the last few thousand years. That veil is none other than the Ego—our age-old Enemy within, who is but a shadow of our true Self—the usurper of the throne of the King.

Throughout this book, the term "Ego" will be used to refer to an unseen entity that has taken up residence at the basis of our minds. It is important to note at the outset that this term will not be used in Sigmund Freud's sense. Rather, it will be used to describe a vacuous entity, ultimately a non-entity, which has usurped the place of our true Self.

Just as darkness is the absence of light, emptiness is the absence of fullness, and ignorance is the absence of knowledge, so also, the Ego represents the non-Self—the absence of the Self. It is nothing more than a veil of pure ignorance, a veil of empty darkness, located at the basis of the mind, which hides from us the true nature of the Self.

The coming global transformation is designed to lift this veil from our awareness, both individually and collectively, so that the light of the Self, the light of pure knowledge, might shine forth. That is the true Apocalypse, the Final Event, which will usher in a new Golden Age for all mankind.

## Paradise

Virtually every ancient culture around the world, even at the very beginnings of recorded history, looked back with nostalgia at an earlier period, lost in the mists of time, when human beings on earth enjoyed an almost divine existence and lived in a natural paradise filled with the presence of God.

The Judeo-Christian tradition describes this time as the Garden of Eden, when Adam and Eve, the prototypical man and woman, lived in innocence and peace.

The Egyptian tradition refers to the *zep tepi*—the first time, when the gods walked the earth. The Vedic tradition calls it *satya yuga*—the Age of Truth—when the sons and daughters of immortality roamed the forests and plains. In the Greek and Roman traditions it was known as the Golden Age.

Hesiod, a Greek poet, who lived in the latter part of the eighth century BC, described the characteristics of the Golden Age in his poetic treatise *Works and Days*.[2] In summary, he said:

> The Golden Age is the only age that falls within the rule of Cronus. It is said that men lived among the gods and freely mingled with them. Peace and harmony prevailed during this age. Humans did not have to work to feed themselves, for the earth provided food in abundance. They lived to a very old age but with a youthful appearance and eventually died peacefully. Their spirits live on as "guardians."[3]

It is easy for modern scientific man to dismiss these myths of an earlier Golden Age, when men walked among the gods and enjoyed a semi-divine existence in an earthly paradise, as products of mythical fantasy.

The human mind has a natural tendency to romanticize the past: to remember the good things and forget the bad. So it is easy to assume that these myths are but romanticized memories of the ancient past. But my own experience has confirmed to my satisfaction that there is more truth to the myths than one might imagine.

Even my earliest experience of the divine, experienced in the lap of Nature so long ago, tells me that the awakened human soul is inherently capable of a semi-divine existence without any of the trappings of modern civilization.

Then there is the question of the "gods." Who were the gods that mingled with our ancestors? In my opinion, this is more a question of direct experience than theology. The ancients tended to view anyone or anything that manifests the presence of God as a "god." This could even include an enlightened human being. For example, consider the following passage taken from the ancient Hermetic texts:

> These men got a share of gnosis; they received [the divine] mind (*nous*), and so became complete men…these, my son, in comparison with the others, are as immortal gods to mortal men. They embrace in their own mind all things that are, the things on earth and the things in heaven, and even what is above heaven, if there is aught above heaven, and raising themselves to that height, they see the Good…. Such, my son, is the work that mind does; it throws open the way to knowledge of things divine, and enables us to apprehend God.[4]

It is also likely that the term "god" was applied to the divine messengers, the great denizens of heaven, who descended to earth and manifested the glory of God in their presence.

In my own experience, I have come to understand that the great being, who descended from the sky and made manifest the glory of God to me that day on the river bank, was, and is, not the Supreme Being, whom we call God.

This was a divine messenger, a great and enlightened denizen of heaven, who was filled with the glory of God. Using the criteria of the ancients, such beings could certainly be called "gods," but they could also be called the "angels" of God. Having been graced by encounters with such beings myself, I see no reason why our ancient ancestors could not have done so as well.

Finally, it is abundantly clear to me that if the majority of human beings on earth were to attain the type of awakened consciousness that I was granted that glorious day, when, filled with overflowing love and compassion, I saw everything within nature, animate and inanimate, as my younger brothers and sisters, then there is no doubt that we, as a species, can live in peace and harmony not only with Nature, but also with each other.

In other words, my own direct experience has convinced me of the truth in the testimony of the ancients throughout the world that there really was a Golden Age that existed on earth long ago.

I join in the concern of many today, that having fallen from that state, we have forgotten how to commune with the Divine, immanent within us and in all existing beings, and that we appear hell-bent on destruction of our planet and ourselves.

The purpose of this book is to share my firm and grounded conviction that we will recover our innocence, become children of God once again, and that a new Golden Age is just over the horizon.

Just as when approaching the sea, one can sense and smell its proximity even though the waves have not yet been seen, so also, many intuitives now sense that the dawn of a new Golden Age, a new Age of Truth, is close at hand.

With this book, I join in the choir of many heralds who have arisen in the pre-dawn hours to awaken others and deliver the message that a new day is dawning. In other words, this book is designed to be a wake-up call.

The old and decrepit body of the phoenix is about to be immolated in the sacred fire. But out of the glowing ashes of its sacrificial body, that is, out of the sparks of divinity that lie latent within each human soul, a new body of the phoenix, filled with the light of pure knowledge and imbued with eternal Life, will arise.

## Paradise Lost

All of recorded history tells us that we have been at war with ourselves since the very beginnings of human civilization. It teaches us that, when given the chance, the Ego, the source of all corruption, will raise its ugly head and take over.

The Ego is driven to seek power and control and is willing to use any means at its disposal to obtain and keep it. Because it has infected the human soul for at least the last four- to five-thousand years, that is, for the entire duration of recorded history, we readily accept the truth of Lord Acton's oft-quoted statement: *Power tends to corrupt, and absolute power corrupts absolutely.*

Recorded history repeatedly tells the tragic tale of powerful leaders who have rallied or conscripted the people under their charge to beat their plowshares into swords and follow them on the road to conquest; to risk their own lives in the roiling storm clouds of war; to engage in the wholesale slaughter of men, women, children, and animals; and to enslave the conquered.

Beyond any doubt, the twentieth century stands as the most barbaric century in recorded history. It has been estimated that some 196-million people lost their lives in the last century due to wars and programs of mass genocide that we unleashed upon each other. This figure represents more death and destruction than the sum total of all that came before.

Today, in the twenty-first century, though mostly hidden from sight, the practice of slavery still persists. However, the chains of iron and steel have largely been replaced by contractual chains, enslaving in debt nations, peoples, and individuals.

In our world, where many large corporations and banking institutions have larger economies than entire nations, economic warfare has trumped military warfare. Now whole nations can be reduced to ruin by the flick of a pen or the stroke of a computer.

Sadly, the natural paradise of our planet has been significantly diminished, and what remains is rapidly disappearing. We have polluted our rivers and seas, consumed vast forests, decimated thousands of species of plants and animals, and scarred the landscape with belching factories and smog-filled cities.

The worship of God has been replaced by the worship of money, our new false god, and the sacred temples of the past have given way to the vast skyscrapers of today, devoted to this new god. In these hollow monuments to mammon, people labor under the yoke of their corporate managers, often wondering if they are living to work, or working to live.

This new false god, worshipped by the Ego, is not benevolent.

Rather, it inspires insatiable greed, war, and destruction. Through the insidious influence of the Ego, enamored of this false god, we have entered into a perpetual state of war and appear hell-bent on destroying the earth.

Exhausts have ruined the air; pesticides, chemical fertilizers, and mono-crops have depleted once fertile land; and genetically modified plants are now killing the bees. In short, like drunken drivers, we are careening along the road to self-destruction—and the earth resembles a paradise no more.

## The Blame Game

It is clear to most of us that something is radically wrong. In response, we engage in the blame game, accusing various individuals and groups of being responsible for our woes. For example, take the current economic crisis.

In the United States, Democrats blame Republicans, Republicans blame Democrats, and both are blaming the bankers and their Wall Street collaborators. In the world at large, nations are blaming each other. Round and round the blame game goes and where it will end nobody knows.

To the ordinary person on the street, the whole thing seems incomprehensible. The economic, corporate, political, and social systems of the world are just too vast and complex to properly evaluate. Nevertheless, there is a growing consensus that the system has gone wrong, and that we may be too late to prevent it from self-destructing.

## What is the Solution?

But what are we to do? Opposing parties advocate two differing approaches. One approach involves replacing the people in charge, while the other involves changing the system itself. Can we really believe either of these will work?

The first approach suggests that if we can find really "good" people, who will serve the best interests of the people under their charge, rather than their own self-interests, then this would solve the problem. While this might help in the short term, in the long term, others will replace those given the reins of power—and it would be just a matter of time before the "good" people were replaced by "bad" people, who would abuse the system to benefit themselves and their cronies at the cost of others. Consequently, we would soon find ourselves back in the same situation as before. So, no, this is not an adequate long-term solution.

What about changing the system itself? The second approach suggests that if we created a new, fair, and equitable system, which levels the playing field or places more rigorous checks and balances on the people in charge, then they would be prevented from abusing their power. Surely that would work—or would it?

Unfortunately, this, too, has been tried before—and it doesn't prevent corruption. To cite a concrete example, let us look at our own country, the United States of America. Our founding fathers, keenly aware of the problem, carefully installed safeguards to limit the power of the system of Federal Government, by providing various checks and balances on those in charge, so that the inalienable rights of the people would be protected. The Constitution and Bill of Rights were designed to be bulwarks against the abuse of power.

This worked fine for a while, and the new republic served as a shining example of freedom to the people of the world for at least one-hundred years. Millions of religious and political refugees, oppressed by despots abroad, sought refuge in the new nation—and the people flourished.

Nevertheless over time, the system itself became corrupted. Today parts of the Constitution have been abandoned, and the inalienable rights of the people are progressively being eroded in the name of National Security. Like a parasitic cancer, the Federal Government has grown to enormous size and now consumes the lion's share of the people's wealth in the form of burdensome taxes and multi-generational debt.

It was a laudable experiment, but in the end it couldn't be sustained. The Ego, the source of all corruption in the human soul, eventually found a way to divert and rig the system to selfish and unjust ends.

Given the corrupting influence of the Ego, any new system, no matter how ideal, will deteriorate over time. Is this our fate—to be plagued by corruption and eternally at war with ourselves? Are we doomed to self-destruction?

## The End Times

At this stage in human history we have come to the end of our rope. The Ego, the monster in the basement, who has moved upstairs and is now wrecking our house, intends to demolish it completely. The signs are all around us. Its evil eye is staring at us from every direction. We are in the death throes of the world as we know it, and our way of life is about to be changed radically and irrevocably. The End Times are upon us.

This is not an accident. It is not an unforeseen event. Indeed, it was destined to happen. The difficult time in which we now live has been foretold by prophecies since time immemorial.

In order to pave the way for the Golden Age to come, the Ego, which has taken root in virtually every human soul, must first be weakened and humbled. This will be accomplished for us; we will not have to do anything at all. The Ego will weaken and humble itself.

The Ego is bent on self-destruction and the institutions under its control—all of the social, political, corporate, and economic institutions that now dominate the world—are about to self-destruct. The entire global system, infected by the disease called Ego, has bad blood, filled with corruption. That bad blood is money and its corruption is debt. This is the corruption that will destroy the world, *as we know it*.

Although it is easy to blame the leaders of these institutions for our collective woes, one should not be so quick to cast stones, for we are all caught up in this together. We are all caught up in the tentacles of the Beast, the great Ego, whose lust for greed and power knows no bounds.

We might despise the policies of our social institutions, but we should not despise the souls of those who implement them. They deserve compassion for they have been deceived, and they know not what they do.

In the process of wrecking our world, the Ego will destroy its own possessions; it will destroy its own wealth and power, and as a result, it will become weakened and humbled.

Although this may result in hardship and suffering, it will also present each of us, even those in charge of our social, political, and economic institutions, with an unparalleled opportunity.

When the Ego becomes humbled and weakened, we will all

have the opportunity to seek refuge in the silent darkness of our own souls. There we will each have to confront our individual Ego, the Enemy within, and banish it. Then all the tumult will stop and we will find "peace at last, peace at last, thank God Almighty, peace at last."

Those who choose to take this path—to confront the Enemy within and to give up all forms of outer strife—will be given the keys to the Kingdom, and the meek shall inherit the earth.

Although this great opportunity will be offered to all, each of us is endowed with free will. Those who choose to keep up the "good fight," by doing battle with the outer demons of their imagination, wreaking death and destruction upon their fellow men, will simply destroy themselves. Their souls will be banished from the earth for thousands of years to come.

The prophecies, the vision, and the guidance are clear: the destroyers will be destroyed, and the nourishers will be nourished. As a result, the coming times are critical; they will test the mettle of our souls. To survive and flourish, to enter the gates of paradise, each soul must make the choice to confront the Enemy within and reduce it to a mere nothingness.

In truth, there is no need for any death and destruction. Each and every one of us has the innate potential to make the right choice—to go within, banish our age-old Enemy, and then surrender our individual will to universal divine will. In this sense, we are responsible for our own individual destinies. But our collective destiny, the destiny of the world, is etched in stone, and there is nothing that we can do to stop it.

In time, the outer turmoil and strife will come to an end and a great silence will descend upon the earth. Then a Miracle will happen. Through the agency of our own immortal Self, through the ever-present grace of God, the veil of darkness will be lifted from our collective awareness, and the light of the Self will shine forth in the souls of all who remain.

This is the Final Event—the Apocalypse—that will usher in the dawn of a new Golden Age, a new Age of Truth, for all humanity. There is no greater blessing than this. Out of the ashes of our fallen world, a new world, much more glorious than before, will be resurrected, and our souls will be corrupted no more.

But there is more. In times to come, our resurrected souls, like the risen phoenix, will ascend on wings of fire into the starry heavens. We will climb the divine ladder and mount the stairway to the sky. Rising above this world, we will eventually obtain full immortality in the bosom of the infinite. Take heart and have no fear, for despite all outward appearances, something *very* Good is about to happen.

# 2. CYCLES OF TIME

## The Unique Character of our Time

In the larger picture, the Apocalypse, or lifting of the veil, is not a singular, but a cyclic event, one that has happened before and will happen again. Similar events took place approximately 13,000, 26,000, 39,000, and 52,000 years ago, and another such event will occur approximately 13,000 years from now.

The collective consciousness of our planet is governed by 13,000-year cycles of time, which are built into the very fabric of the universe. At the beginning of each cycle, the earth and all its inhabitants, including the minerals, plants, and animals, experience a Golden Age, when the hidden mysteries of the universe are revealed, and life on earth is transformed once again into Paradise.

In each such age God's divine messengers descend to earth. They come to set all beings in proper order and to nourish the earth with their divine presence. Some 52,000 years ago, at the dawn of a previous Golden Age, they infused their life-giving energy into the hominid species called homo-sapiens-sapiens, which was destined to become the dominant species on our planet.

The veil of darkness was removed and light of the Self was kindled in the souls of the newly upgraded species, and, as a result, they became enlightened human beings. These were our ancient ancestors—the ancestors of every human being who now walks the face of the earth.

This marked the dawn of the first epochal day of enlightened human existence on earth. But over the long course of time, the darkness returned, and our ancestors devolved into little more than primitive savages, struggling to survive under harsh environmental conditions.

Then a new Apocalypse occurred, and once again the veil of darkness was removed. Another Golden Age ensued, and our ancestors became enlightened once more.

In this manner, over the course of the last 52,000 years as a species, we have experienced four previous Golden Ages, all of which have faded into the mists of time. We now stand poised to experience one again. In spite of the deplorable current situation, the veil of darkness will soon be removed again, and the earth, once more, will come to resemble Paradise.

However, the coming global transformation is unique, distinct from any that has come before. Some 52,000 years ago, when the light of the Self first dawned in the human soul, we were but infants and over the course of the intervening years, we have gone through our childhood.

During times of darkness, we imagined monsters in the night and fought amongst ourselves like children without any sense of moral responsibility. All of this took place during the first epochal day and night of our existence on earth—one that lasted for 52,000 years.

The unending turmoil that has embroiled humanity during the past few thousand years is a sign of our collective puberty. We are about to emerge as adult citizens of the universe—capable of genuine "co-creation." With the dawn of the coming Golden Age, we will simultaneously experience the dawn of our second epochal day on earth, and we will come forth into the light of that day with greater maturity than we possessed before.

Among other things, this means that we will act as responsible adults, even during times of darkness. The cycles of time will continue to occur as they have before. Light will be followed by darkness, and darkness by light. But unlike children, we will no longer imagine demons in the darkness, and we will never again fall prey to our age-old Enemy. Other challenges and victories will be ours to face.

We thus stand on the threshold of a whole new world—an adult world, in which we will become true citizens of the universe, capable of exploring all its marvelous wonders in a responsible civic manner.

The earth is now filled with almost seven billion people, because human souls have thronged here to witness this event. Souls have clamored to be born on earth at this time, under any condition, just to obtain this glorious opportunity.

Those who take advantage of this opportunity, and make the right choice, will be elevated to the status of spiritually mature adults. We will then be accepted into the company of the great denizens of heaven, as their equals. We will then become, like them, co-creators employed in the service of the Creator.

# The Precession of Equinoxes

Just like the cycles of day and night, or the cycles of the seasons, the long 13,000-year cycles, which govern the rise and fall of consciousness on earth, are built into the fabric of the universe and intimately related to astronomical phenomena. More specifically, they are related to the precession of equinoxes.

The precession of the equinoxes, based on astronomical observation, results from a cyclic change in the orientation of the earth's rotational axis.

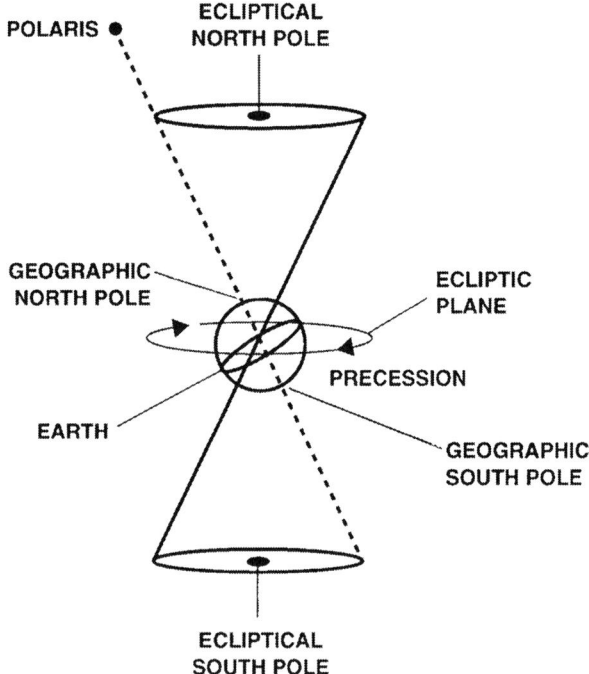

**Figure 1 - The Precession of the Equinoxes**

The timing of the cycle is determined by observing the change in the position of the sun relative to the fixed stars at dawn on the vernal equinox each year. From the perspective of an earth-based observer, the sun appears to shift its position by a very small, but perceptible, amount relative to the fixed stars each year, as if it follows a circular trajectory.

Careful observations reveal that the sun moves through about 50.3 seconds of arc per year, or 1 degree every 71.6 years. A complete revolution through 360 degrees thus spans a period of 25,771.5 years. One half of that period is equal to 12,885.75 years, which can be rounded off to 12,885.8.

Modern astrophysicists do not accord the precession of the equinoxes any special significance. They view it as part of the mechanical operation of the universe. But the magi, sages, and seers of most ancient cultures realized the great importance of this cycle, and understood it to be profoundly related to the changes in qualities in human consciousness on earth.

However, the precession of equinoxes is not a causal factor in the evolution of consciousness. It is merely an indicator, a correlate, which can be used to mark the phases of evolution over the long course of time. It is the will of God, operating non-locally throughout the entire universe, which causes the evolution of consciousness.

Just as the consciousness of a human being is linked with the behavior of the human body, so also, the consciousness of the planetary being is linked with the behavior of its planetary body. Thus, the changing orientation of the earth's axis of rotation correlates with the changing consciousness of the earth.

## The Evolution of Consciousness

Our local universe is part of "the body" of a vast divine being, made in the image of God, a being who is a creative representative of God throughout the full extent of Creation.[5] This body extends far beyond the boundaries of our visible universe. All the planets, stars, and galaxies that twinkle in the night sky are parts of this vast universal body whose consciousness pervades all space, including intergalactic space.

Our planet is but a tiny part of that vast universal body. The consciousness of the earth and all its life forms is not only correlated with the precession of the equinoxes, it is also linked with everything else in the universe.

Such a conclusion is inevitable if one accepts the fundamental premise that everything in creation is a product of consciousness—a product of the all-pervading field of consciousness called God or the one eternal Self. If all things come from consciousness, then all things must be endowed with consciousness—including the elementary particles.

The consciousness associated with a living being is called the soul, and all souls, from the soul of an elementary particle to the soul of the universe as a whole, follow an evolutionary course of development dictated by the will of God—the one eternal Self of all beings.

The vast universal being, who is created in the image of God, has its own circulatory system, consisting of streams of consciousness that connect all things in creation. The heart of this great being is everywhere—at the center of every atom, at the center of every planet, at the center of every solar system, at the center of every galaxy, and at the center of the universe as a whole. It is into and out of these universal 'hearts' that the streams of consciousness flow.

Like the beating heart of a human being, which sends pulses of blood throughout the human circulatory system, so also, these universal hearts are beating hearts, which send out pulses of consciousness along the streams that constitute the universal circulatory system. These are not sine waves—they are pulses, which suddenly arrive at their destinations and then gradually taper off over time.

Every 13,000 years a major pulse of consciousness, which comes from the very center of the universe, washes over our planet, and like a tidal wave that elevates all boats, this pulse elevates the consciousness of all beings on earth.

Just as fresh blood pumped from the human heart serves to nourish the cells and tissues of the human body, so also, the fresh pulse of consciousness pumped from the universal heart serves to nourish the bodies of all beings on earth. It also serves to remove the veil of ignorance that has darkened all souls since the last pulse, some 13,000 years before.

Thus, at the end of each 13,000-year cycle, when consciousness is at its lowest ebb and the world in its darkest hour, a new tidal wave washes over our planet, and all beings on earth suddenly attain an elevated state of consciousness, very different from that which they had before. In this elevated state the deeper mysteries of the universe are revealed and all beings on earth become consciously connected, such that a state of oneness arises throughout Nature.

Following each such tidal wave, there is a long and gradual decline in the consciousness of the earth, during which the deeper mysteries of the universe become progressively concealed from the awareness of all beings.

However, this is not just an endless round of circular repetition. Our planetary consciousness is shaped through an evolutionary spiral, and that spiral is taking us somewhere—toward the full potential of the human race.

Our journey so far has served an integrative purpose. Towards the beginning of each cycle, we have to rely upon our intuitive and spiritual faculties, and toward the end we have to rely upon our empirical and rational faculties.

The goal is to have both faculties fully developed and functioning simultaneously—such that our whole brain, our whole consciousness, is utilized to the fullest. Only then will we attain our full potential. That is our destiny, both individually and collectively, and we are moving toward it through an evolutionary sequence of cycles, each of which spans many thousands of years.

## The 52,000-Year Cycle

During each complete precessional cycle, the sun traverses all twelve signs of the zodiac, which can be compared to the twelve hours on the face of a cosmic clock.

In this analogy, the cusp of Leo marks the twelve o'clock point, while the cusp of Aquarius marks the six o'clock point. The position of the sun on the vernal equinox can then be compared to the cosmic hour hand, which tells us the time indicated by the clock.

At the present moment in history, the hour hand points to 6 am on the cosmic clock. In other words, we are about to experience the dawn of a new epochal day.

The previous dawn, which began the first day of human life on earth, occurred 52,000 years ago. Since that time, the hour hand has made two revolutions round the face of the clock, corresponding to one 12-hour day and one 12-hour night.

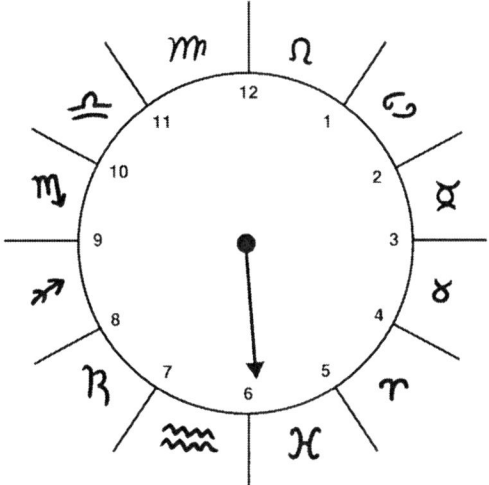

**Figure 2 - The Cosmic Clock**

The most important hours on the cosmic clock are those that correspond to dawn (6 am), noon (12 pm), dusk (6 pm), and midnight (12 am). These times mark the end of one 13,000-year cycle and the beginning of another. It is at these times that a fresh pulse of consciousness washes over our planet, and a new Golden Age begins.

In this context, the four 13,000 year sub-cycles that make up the larger 52,000 year cycle, can be compared to four six-hour watches during a complete 24-hour period of day and night.

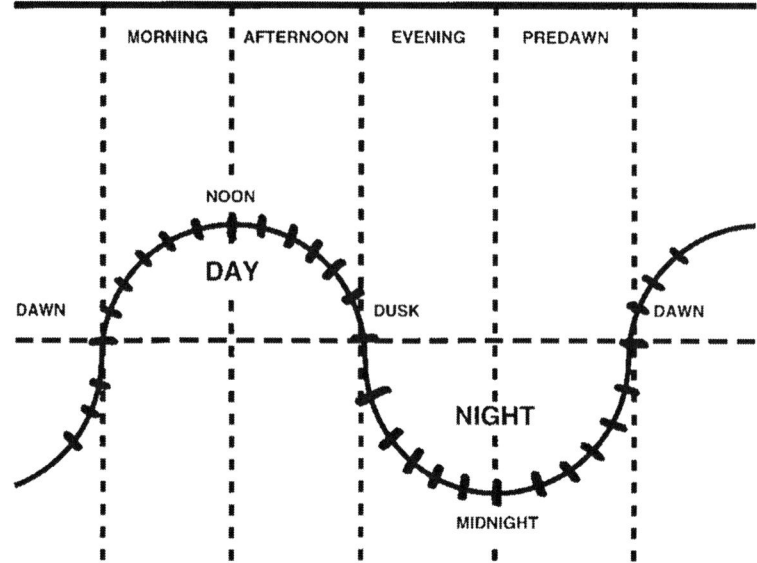

**Figure 3 - The Epochal Day and Night**

Just as the quality of morning is different from that of the afternoon, and the evening differs from the pre-dawn period, so also, the qualities of the four six-hour watches of the cosmic clock are different one from the other. During these watches the qualities of consciousness display their different characteristics.

During the period called "morning" our planetary consciousness is most fresh and alive, and during the period called "evening," it is most dull and tired. Midnight on the cosmic clock occurred about 13,000 years ago. During the pre-dawn period our collective awareness began to stir, and we are about to wake up to the dawn of a whole new day.

It has been 52,000 years since we experienced our last epochal dawn. This marked the beginning of our first morning on earth. We are about to experience another such dawn, which will mark the beginning of our second morning on earth. This means that the coming Golden Age will be especially vibrant and alive.

Over the course of the last 13,000 years, we have made an important step in our evolutionary development. We have stepped out of the dark primeval forests into the light of civilization and have begun to use our powers of reason to develop advanced forms of physical science and material technology.

Just as we do not allow children to handle guns and automobiles lest they hurt themselves and others, so also, during the early stages of our development we were not allowed to develop advanced material technologies lest we destroy ourselves.

Only recently, in the last few minutes before the dawn, were these things given to us, because we are about to reach an age when we can use them properly and safely, not for self-destruction, but for the nourishment of all things in creation.

There is no doubt that, if left unchecked, we would use our advanced technologies to destroy ourselves. For this reason these things were withheld and only given to us at the last minute, just before the dawn, on the threshold of our awakening as spiritually mature adults—true citizens of the universe.

We are accustomed to thinking of our technological discoveries as pure inventions of the human mind, which is only partly true. For it is also true that all of the most important inventions of the human mind have been inspired by our unseen divine benefactors, who can not only read every human thought, but also inspire human thought at will—from any distance.

As conscious beings, we have free will. Over the course of the last few thousand years we have exercised our free will toward the destruction of our fellow human beings and the other creatures with which we share this beautiful planet. All of that is about to change. We are about to become nourishers, rather than destroyers—and not a moment too soon.

The unique feature of the coming Golden Age will be the coexistence of advanced spiritual consciousness along with advanced material technologies. This will be the age when we finally are admitted into the larger society of intelligent beings throughout the universe, some of whom are much more advanced than ourselves.

It will also be the age when physical science is transformed into spiritual science—a genuine science of consciousness, which will open up new technologies, both mental and physical, beyond our wildest dreams. This is not mere speculation; the keys to such a science have already been made available and placed in safe-keeping, and the vision of the future laid out in this book is authorized from on High.

Needless to say the coming global transformation will not be trivial. To go from where we are now to where we soon shall be, a radical transformation in virtually every aspect of human life—social, economical, political, intellectual, and spiritual—is required. In all likelihood, the transition will be turbulent, chaotic, and even painful.

Like an infant being squeezed through the birth canal, our birth process as spiritual adults will be accompanied by trauma. This book is being written in the hope that it will offer some insights to minimize the pain and to share a glimpse of the glorious light that lies at the end of the dark tunnel—the spiritual birth canal.

The old saying that the darkest hour of night is just before dawn also holds true in our current situation. The immediate future does indeed appear frightening, but we must now remember the inspiring words of President Roosevelt: "The only thing we have to fear is fear itself." Truer words have never been spoken.

# 3. THE AGES OF MAN

## Oedipus the King

In many respects, the coming global transformation will be tragic. Many of the things that we have come to cherish and hold dear will be destroyed or taken away from us, and the tighter we cling to those things, the more we will suffer.

However, there is nothing we can do to avoid the transformation, because it is foreordained; it is our destiny, foretold by sages and seers in widely varying religious traditions throughout history.

In this regard, light can be shed on the coming social tragedy by Sophocles' tragedy *Oedipus the King*, composed in the fifth century BC.

Before his birth, the oracle of Delphi prophesized that Oedipus, the son of the king of Thebes, would kill his own father and marry his own mother. Everyone informed of this tragic destiny did everything they could to avoid it. The King, Oedipus's Father, had him removed to be murdered. Instead he was abandoned, discovered and adopted by a neighboring ruler. All parties involved in the story exerted their free will to avert the destiny, but despite this, all of their choices only served to deliver Oedipus to his tragic end.

Similarly, the coming social tragedy was prophesized long ago. Even today, as we grow closer to the event, many warn of our impending doom. But as in the tragedy of Oedipus, those involved in the current tragedy are powerless to stop it. In spite of the best efforts of our leaders to deliver us from it, their actions will only serve to bring about our tragic fate.

The coming transformation lies beyond the control of any individual or institution. A part of our collective destiny, it is being brought about *by the influence of time*, working through every individual and institution on earth. But unlike the story of Oedipus, our tragedy has a golden lining: it will deliver us to a new Age of Truth for all mankind.

## The Riddle of the Ages

The tragedy of Oedipus revolves around a mysterious Sphinx, a word of Greek, not Egyptian, origin. In Egypt, the Sphinx was called *Shesep-ankh*—"the living image" or "the image endowed with eternal life." After the conquest of Egypt by Alexander the Great in 332 BCE, the Greeks renamed the mysterious Egyptian monument, previously called *Shesep-ankh,* the Sphinx.

According to Greek myth, the Sphinx, a hybrid feminine creature, guarded the entrance to the city of Thebes. Ares, the god of war sent her from her Ethiopian homeland to plague the city of Thebes with her riddle:

> Which creature in the morning goes on four legs, at mid-day on two, and in the evening upon three, and the more legs it has, the weaker it be?

Those who failed to answer the riddle correctly were strangled to death. For this reason, the word "sphinx" is thought to be derived from the verbal root *sphíngo*, meaning "to strangle". The Sphinx is often depicted with the body of a lioness, perhaps because the big cats tend to strangle their victims.

After unknowingly killing his own father, Oedipus ventured to the kingdom of Thebes, where he encountered the Sphinx. His mother, the queen of Thebes, distraught over the loss of her husband, and wishing to rid her kingdom of the Sphinx, offered her hand in marriage to anyone who could answer its riddle and thus banish the beast from the kingdom.

Upon being asked the riddle, Oedipus correctly answered "Man." Sure enough, man crawls on all fours as a babe, walks on two feet as an adult, and then hobbles with a cane in old age. The mysterious riddle of the Sphinx thus pertains to the "ages of man." The tragedy of Oedipus, on the other hand, deals with the relationship between free will and destiny over the course of the "life of man." These things are related.

According to some accounts, there was a second riddle proffered by the Sphinx: "There are two sisters: one gives birth to the other and she, in turn, gives birth to the first. Who are these sisters?" The answer is "day and night," both of which are feminine words in Greek.

One thus finds that, at least in the Greek mind, the Sphinx proffered riddles related to the ages of man and the cycles of time, which can be described in terms of day and night. When Oedipus finally solved these riddles, he fulfilled his own destiny—by marrying his own mother, from whom he had been separated since birth.

As tragic as it might sound, his marriage serves as a potent symbol. Upon realizing his own destiny, Oedipus inseminated the womb from which he was born—a symbol of cyclic return.

In the Greek mind the Sphinx thus carried a variety of connotations related to: (i) the ages of man, (ii) cycles of time, (iii) the relationship between free will and destiny, and (iv) cyclic return.

The Ptolemies, Greek pharaohs of Egypt, installed by Alexander the Great, renamed the mysterious monument the "Sphinx." This renaming was non-trivial. The astute Greeks recognized the Egyptian monument as enshrining in stone significant elements of the myth of Oedipus. My conclusion is that the Sphinx was designed to be a "living image" of the current 13,000-year cycle, which is now about to end. This is supported by the following indications.

The Sphinx, aligned on a true East-West axis, faces due East. At this critical moment in time, at dawn on the vernal equinox, the sun appears to rise in the first degree of the sign of Aquarius, whose symbol is a man pouring liquid from cup. The Sphinx has the head of a man—as such it faces its own image in the East.

On that same, first day of spring, at that same moment of sunrise, the cusp of Leo is setting in the West—behind the Sphinx. The symbol of Leo is the Lion and the body of the Sphinx, including its hind part, is that of a lion. The rear of the Sphinx thus faces its own image in the West. Therefore, the Sphinx presents a living image of the heavens in our current epoch.

This indicates to me that the Sphinx was designed to endure through all the ages in order to serve as a prophetic marker for the end of the current cycle—when the glory of the ancient spiritual wisdom, which has since been lost, would be revived, and a new Golden Age, a new "first time," would dawn once again on earth.

In this sense, the Sphinx represents a riddle of the ages, which is effectively solved by the current moment in the precessional cycle. With this solution, we, like Oedipus, are now ready to meet our destiny, which will come to pass no matter how much we try to avoid it.

## The Four Ages of Man

The long 13,000-year cycle consists of four ages. In the context of human life on earth these can be called the "Four Ages of Man." My intuitive insight regarding these ages comes from the sources described in the introductory section of this book, supplemented by intellectual inquiry.

The model of the ages developed on the basis of these insights has powerful predictive ability. But before we discuss this model, lets first review the teachings of the ancients.

Hesiod, the eighth-century BC Greek poet, described the Ages of Man in his poetic treatise *Works and Days*.[6] He outlined four ages called the Golden Age, the Silver age, the Bronze Age, and the Iron Age. The Roman poet Ovid narrates a similar myth of four ages in his poem *Metamorphoses*.[7]

In the writings of Hesiod, the Golden Age is described as a distant age when men enjoyed a semi-divine existence in the presence of the gods. During the Silver Age that followed, men began to engage in strife with one another. In the Bronze Age, life was hard, and war became the purpose and passion of men. The Iron Age was described as a despicable time.

> During this [Iron] age humans live an existence of toil and misery. Children dishonor their parents, brother fights with brother and the social contract between guest and host is forgotten. During this age might makes right, and bad men use lies to be thought good. At the height of this age, humans no longer feel shame or indignation at wrongdoing; babies will be born with grey hair and the gods will have completely foresaken humanity: "there will be no help against evil."

Does this sound familiar? It should, because it provides a fairly accurate description of what has been happening on earth for quite some time.

In the ancient Vedic tradition a similar set of four ages were described, called the four *yugas*, where the word *yuga*, meaning "age," comes from the Sanskrit root *yuj* = to yoke or join. As in the Greek and Roman traditions, the four ages involved a progressive decline in spiritual awareness from the first age, called "the Age of Spiritual Truth," to the fourth age, called "the Age of Spiritual Darkness."[8]

The varying lengths of the four Vedic ages constitute increasingly shorter periods of time that in relation to each other display the ratios 4:3:2:1. More specifically, the texts state that the first age spans 4,800 years, the second 3,600 years, the third 2,400 years, and the fourth 1,200 years. Added together, the four ages cover a period of 12,000 years.[9]

However, in addition to four human ages, there were also four celestial ages, which had the same names. To obtain the corresponding celestial ages, each human year is multiplied by a celestial year, which consists of 360 human years. The respective periods of the human and celestial ages, expressed in solar years, are tabulated below.

| Yuga | Human Period | Celestial Period |
|---|---|---|
| First | 4800 | 4800 x 360 = 1,728,000 |
| Second | 3600 | 3600 x 360 = 1,296,000 |
| Third | 2400 | 2400 x 360 = 864,000 |
| Fourth | 1200 | 1200 x 360 = 432,000 |

In many Vedic texts, the celestial ages are given precedence over the human ages, and there is a general view that the celestial ages are of greater importance than the human ages. The reason for this is simple.

The Vedic texts were written by enlightened seers whose awareness embraced all things i.e., "the things on earth and the things in heaven, and even what is above heaven, if there is aught above heaven." This means that their awareness was not restricted to this small planet. Rather, it was cosmic in scope, and for them the celestial ages were more important than the human ages.

In comparison to the mortal souls of today, they were like immortal gods. Even though their feet walked on earth, their minds soared freely in the starry heavens, which were the realms of their direct experience, and they reckoned time in terms of the celestial ages, which pertain to the evolution of consciousness in the greater universe, rather than the human ages, which pertain to the evolution of consciousness on this small planet.

Since then, human awareness has lost its celestial bearings. It has shrunk down in size and scope, and today, the human ages are of greater importance to us than the celestial ages—for they directly bear upon our own destiny, the destiny of every mortal soul on earth.

## Rectified Periods

In what follows I present a rectified theory of the four ages, consistent with the knowledge I have received from my divine benefactors, in whom I have complete confidence.

The *Manu Smriti,* which is the oldest and most authoritative book of Vedic law, whose title means "The Memory of Man," is fairly accurate with regard to both the periods of the four human ages and their ratios. But something has been left out—the ancient text has left out the gaps between the ages.[10]

These are gaps of time, during which the spiritual laws governing the previous age have come to an end, but the new laws governing the subsequent age have not yet arisen.

During these gaps, the compass of human consciousness ceases to be yoked to a particular age and thus loses its bearing. As a result, the gaps between the ages represent periods of relative social chaos, during which the old order dies out and the seeds of a new order are sown. Those seeds eventually sprout with the dawn of the subsequent age.

Like the four ages themselves, the four gaps also display the ratios 4:3:2:1. More specifically, the four gaps span periods of 384, 288, 192, and 96-years respectively, amounting to an additional 960 years that must be intercalated and included in the overall calculation. Using the rounded numbers of the ancients the complete cycle of human ages thus spans a total of 12,000 + 960 = 12,960 years.

This is approximately equal to one half the precessional cycle, which spans six zodiacal ages, corresponding to six hours on the cosmic clock. Modern astronomical calculations yield the more accurate figure of 12,885.8 years for this same period.

To provide a more accurate accounting of the cycle, the modern astronomical calculation should be used. This requires a rectification of the periods provided by the ancients, such that all the periods are shortened by a factor of .005729 as tabulated below.

| Ages and Gaps | Periods (Total: 12,885.8) |
|---|---|
| **First Age** | 4772.50 |
| First Gap | 381.80 |
| **Second Age** | 3579.40 |
| Second Gap | 286.35 |
| **Third Age** | 2386.25 |
| Third Gap | 190.90 |
| **Fourth Age** | 1193.10 |
| Fourth Gap | 95.50 |

The system of ages and gaps presented above is unique, *for it directly ties the periods to one half the precession cycle*. This is the **first key** to a full rectification of the cycle.

# The Linchpin

The **second key** lies in determining any one of many possible linchpins, a peg, which will indicate the dating of all the ages. What is required is pinpointing a significant event, tied to a particular date, which can, in turn, be associated with a particular point in the cycle. This event can then serve as the linchpin, on the basis of which the beginning and ending dates of the four ages and their associated gaps can be determined.

The most carefully and completely documented period in human history is the twentieth century. Moreover, the twentieth century, clearly, represents a unique period in human history. It was marked by the most rapid and far-reaching changes in social organization, commerce, transportation, science, technology, population, and warfare, which have ever occurred in recorded history.

This description corresponds precisely to what has long been predicted for the end of the cycle, corresponding to the final 95.5-year gap that lies between the end of Age of Spiritual Darkness and the beginning of the new Age of Truth. It seems reasonable, therefore, to look for a particular event during the twentieth century that could be linked with the starting point of this gap.

Because the major changes in social history over the course of the twentieth century were largely man-made, one must look to the engine that drove, fed, and largely controlled the direction of human endeavors during the century. Indeed, it is common knowledge that money is that engine. More than anything else, money is the driving force as well as the very lifeblood of modern society.

At the present time, the most dominant form of money is the

United States dollar, which was adopted as the standard unit of international exchange in 1944 during the Bretton Woods Conference. Is there any singular event linked to the dollar that might be viewed as kicking off the rapid and turbulent transformations of corporate, national, and international society during the twentieth century? In fact, there is.

The amount of dollars in circulation is determined and controlled by the Federal Reserve System, which Congress, reluctantly and somewhat unwittingly, authorized and established by the Federal Reserve Act, signed into law by Woodrow Wilson on December 23, 1913. Some two months later, in February 1914, Congress passed the Federal Income Tax Act, and approximately six months later, the assassination of the Austrian monarch Archduke Ferdinand occurred, initiating the First World War.

Because neither the collection of taxes nor the waging of war are possible without money, and because the Federal Reserve System became the sole creator and regulator of money in the form of US dollars from the time of its inception, it seems reasonable to choose December 23, 1913, the date of the Fed's creation, as the linchpin that marks the start of the rapidly changing and turbulent period that corresponds to the final gap.

## Rectified Dates

Using the proposed linchpin, the beginning and ending dates of the pertinent periods are given in rounded numbers below.

The dates are given for the year in which the periods begin and end, not the fractional values of those years. Our primary interest is the final gap. The more precise calculations suggest that this period should last for 95.549 years. Starting from the date of the linchpin, or December 23, 1913, it follows that the final gap should end in early June 2009. This is just couple of months from the time of this writing. What does this date represent?

| Ages and Gaps | Rectified Periods (Total: 12,888.8) | Rectified Dates (Gregorian) |
|---|---|---|
| **First Age** | 4772.50 | 110876-6104 BC |
| First Gap | 381.80 | 6103-5722 BC |
| **Second Age** | 3579.40 | 5722-2143 BC |
| Second Gap | 286.35 | 2142-1857 BC |
| **Third Age** | 2386.25 | 1856 BC-530 AD |
| Third Gap | 190.90 | 529-720 AD |
| **Fourth Age** | 1193.10 | 720-1913 AD |
| Fourth Gap | 95.50 | 1913-2009 AD |

## The Purifying Influence of Time

It is my understanding that the month of June 2009 pinpoints the time frame in which the current cycle will end and the new cycle will begin. However, it will begin with a seven-year period of purification, known as the Tribulation, which will be brought about by the purifying influence of time.

The purifying influence of time is designed to infuse divine consciousness into human consciousness. During the period of purification, all the filth and corruption accumulated in our collective psyche and current world system will be purged. This can be compared to a period of withdrawal.

Think of a heroin addict starting to undergo withdrawal. Going through the withdrawal period takes several days, during which the patient experiences intense suffering as the toxins are purged from the body. The withdrawal period for our current world system is going to take much longer than that, and the suffering will be far more intense, because we have several thousand years of poisonous toxins stored in our collective psyche.

All transformations involving purification start with pain but end in bliss. The question is: how long will it take for us to get out of the pain and into the bliss? The prophetic answer provided by Daniel 9:29 is a "week" of seven years.[1] However, this seven-year period is divided into two halves of forty-two months each.

## The Forty-Two Stages

The ancient sages of the Vedic, Egyptian, and Judaic traditions shared a common understanding about the path that leads from immortality to mortality, or conversely, from mortality to immortality. In all three cases, it was held that the path consists of forty-two stages.

In my book, *Creating the Soul-Body*, the forty-two stages that constitute this path are described in some detail, drawing upon my own experience as well as the wisdom traditions of the Vedic, Egyptian, and Hebrew sages.

These stages are archetypal. They are built into the overall organization of the universe, but they are also reflected in every major transformation of consciousness, which involves a journey between ignorance and knowledge, mortality and immortality, or bondage and liberation.

Moreover, the forty-two stages were understood in two complementary ways. With respect to time these can be called the descending and ascending phases.

During the descending phase, consciousness descends from immortality into mortality, and during the ascending phase it ascends from mortality to immortality. In both cases, the descent and ascent involves a course of forty-two stages.[2]

With respect to the coming seven-year period of purification, these two phases are represented by two forty-two month periods of 3.5 years each. However, this is but a specific manifestation of a universal archetype, built into the very fabric of the universe.

The ancients recognized this universal archetype. In fact, they mapped it out on their sacred lands and spelled it out in their sacred texts.

For example, in the pre-dynastic period, when the land of Egypt was ruled by the *shemsu-hor*, otherwise known as the mystery teachers of heaven, the land of Egypt was divided up into *forty-two* nomes (minor kingdoms), mapped out along the course of the Nile, so that the kingdom of Egypt as a whole might become an image of heaven.

In this case, the forty-two nomes represent the forty-two stages, while the Nile River represents the stream of consciousness that flows through these forty-two stages. By traversing the Nile from its source toward the sea, the soul symbolically follows the ascending path, and by traversing the Nile from the sea toward its source, the soul symbolically follows the descending path.

The *forty-two* stages were also symbolically represented in *The Egyptian Book of the Dead*. This ancient text tells us that when the soul, seeking immortality, enters into the Hall of Two Truths to undergo final judgment, it must first profess its innocence before a tribunal of *forty-two* judges, by reciting the *forty-two* negative confessions.

In a similar vein, Egyptian myth tells us that the wisdom god Thoth wrote a total of *forty-two* secret books, which were said to contain the knowledge of all that lies between heaven and earth.

In the Hebrew Scriptures, Chapter 33 of the Book of Numbers tells us that the sons of Israel (*ben Israel*) traversed a total of *forty-two* stages on their journey through the wilderness, from Egypt, the land of bondage, to Canaan, the Promised Land, which represents the land of liberation.

Because this is a book of "Numbers," the number of stages is important-and the number of stages counted and recorded at the command of God was forty-two.

The importance of this number is also made apparent in the

Zohar, one of the most authoritative texts in the Jewish tradition of Kabalah. The Zohar tells us that the unique name of God, from which the name of Jehovah was derived, originally consisted of *forty-two* letters, and was thus known as the *forty-two* lettered name of God.

According to traditional sources, this unique name of God is spelled out by the first *forty-two* letters of the book of Genesis. These forty-two letters were assigned "creative potential" both in the world of unification and in the world of diversification.

The tradition of Kabalah also tells us that there are *forty-two* divine emanations.[3] By means of these forty-two emanations the supreme Godhead, known as the Ain, progressively descends into the mortal realms, where divine consciousness assumes the form of mortal beings. This was known as the descending path.

However, by means of these same forty-two emanations, the consciousness of a mortal being has the potential to ascend back to the supreme Godhead. This was known as the ascending path.

In the Vedic tradition, the same *forty-two* stages are described and symbolically represented. Iconographically, the stages are represented by the *forty-two* flames that surround the dancing form of Shiva, the Absolute. Diagrammatically, they are represented by the *forty-two* triangles of the *Shri Yantra,* known as the king of all esoteric diagrams. These *forty-two* outer triangles surround the central forty-third triangle, known as the "bestower of all perfection."[4].

None of this is arbitrary; the *forty-two* stages of the path are archetypal-they characterize all major transformations in consciousness throughout the universe and throughout all time.

In the context of the seven-year period of purification, the descending path is represented by the *first forty-two* months, extending from June 2009, to December 2012. During this period, divine consciousness will progressively descend into human consciousness.

However, during this period the Ego will hold sway over the Self. This first forty-two month period is alluded to in the Book of Revelation, which states:

> "Who is like the Beast? Who can fight against it?" The Beast was allowed to mouth bombast and blasphemy, and was given the right to reign for forty-two months.

Here the "Beast" represents our collective Ego, which will be doing everything in its power to maintain control and secure its survival in the face of a rising tide of divine consciousness.

To use an analogy, the seven-year period of purification can be compared to a cosmic battle between the forces of Darkness and Light. During the first half of this period, the forces of Darkness will appear to be stronger than the forces of Light, and no one will be strong enough to challenge the Beast. Hence, the question: "who can fight against it?"

But then, in the middle of the "week" of seven-years, the tide of the battle will turn. From that point forward, the forces of Light will progressively begin to dominate over the forces of Darkness, and in the end, the forces of Darkness will be obliterated.

The second set of forty-two months thus represents the ascending path, during which the Light of the Self will become progressively stronger in our collective awareness.

Although the Light will begin to be seen in the month of December 2012, it will not completely obliterate the Darkness until forty-two months later, corresponding to the month of June, 2016.

These two forty-two month phases correspond to the two phases of the phoenix. During the first phase, the old body of the phoenix is progressively destroyed, and during the second phase, the new body of the phoenix is progressively resurrected.

None of this is arbitrary. The seven-year period of purification has been foretold for thousands of years, and is part of a "divine plan" that will be enacted on earth in the coming few years. The cosmic battle that will take place during this period is symbolically called Armageddon, which represents the final battle between the forces of Darkness and Light.

## The Long Count Mayan Calendar

The mid-point of this seven-year period, which marks the turning point in the cosmic battle is also non-arbitrary. It is well known that the Long Count Mayan calendar will come to an end, or reset to *baktun* 13.0.0.0.0, on December 21, 2012. According to those well-versed in Mayan lore, this date marks a profound transformation in human consciousness, unlike anything that we have ever seen before.

It is my understanding that this will mark the time when the forces of Light, which represent the influence of the Self, will gain superiority over the forces of Darkness, which represent the influence of the Ego, for the first time in thousands of years.

When my own calculations, based on astronomical considerations and intuitive insight regarding the Ages of Man, revealed that the first phase would end in the month of December,

2012, I was astonished at this confluence of ancient prophetic traditions.

In December, 2012, through the grace of God, we will emerge from the "valley of the Shadow of Death" and step into the Light of Life. This marks the beginning of the Final Event—the Apocalypse. Over the ensuing forty-two months the veil of darkness will be progressively removed from human consciousness.

By "progressively," I mean that during this period more and more souls will wake up to the Light of the Self. In the end, all the forces of Darkness will be obliterated. The destroyers will be destroyed and the nourishers—the meek—shall inherit the earth.

Then our mortality will become clothed with immortality, and the words of *First Corinthians* will bear fruit:

> When our mortality has been clothed with immortality, then the saying of the Scripture will come true: "Death has been swallowed up; victory is won! O Death, where is your victory? O Death, where is your sting?"[5]

At that glorious time, the denizens of heaven will rejoice at the dawn of a new epochal day on earth, and a new Golden Age will begin for all mankind.

## The Orion Mystery

The predictions presented above pertain to the future, albeit the near future, and only time will tell if they are correct. But the model also pertains to the past. It predicts that the current cycle began around 10,886 BC. Is there any supporting evidence that this might hold true? In fact, there is. But first, an important refinement within the model must be explained.

According to the Vedic texts,[13] the beginning of each Golden Age, or Age of Truth, is marked by a crescent twilight period, which lasts for 400 years. It is during this period that the new natural laws that govern the Golden Age gradually become manifest in human awareness and society.

To use an analogy, the 400-year twilight period can be compared to the glow on the eastern horizon, prior to the actual rising of the sun. The light is seen at the very beginning of that period, but the full sunshine of the Golden Age, when the light will pervade every aspect of human society, does not occur until the end of that period, some 400 years after the light is first seen. This suggests that the full sunshine of the previous Golden Age occurred around 10,876 - 400 = 10,476 BC. Now lets look at the evidence.

A number of researchers, most notably Graham Hancock and William Bauval, have linked certain monuments in the Nile valley, such as the Pyramids of Giza, with certain star patterns in the sky that occurred around 10,500 BC.

Using computer-generated models, the researchers demonstrated that in that epoch the locations of the three pyramids on the Giza Plateau lined up with the three stars of Orion's belt, and the nearby Nile River lined up with the swath of stars known as the Milky Way, to make manifest a profound sky-ground dualism, or correspondence between heaven and earth, in accordance with the Hermetic dictum, "As above, so below."

In ancient Egypt, the constellation of Orion was identified with Osiris, the first god-king of Egypt, and the Great Pyramid was specifically designed to house the BA (celestial soul) of Osiris. For these reasons, Hancock and Bauval suggested that the monuments are linked with the constellation of Orion in the epoch of 10,500 BC.

They carefully avoided the assertion that the Pyramids were constructed at that time. Rather, they speculated that the monuments were constructed at a much later date, during the Old Kingdom, to commemorate that ancient epoch, which they believed represents the 'first time' (*zep tepi*)—the Egyptian Golden Age.

If the theories of Hancock and Bauval are correct, then this suggests that the ancient Egyptians assigned great significance to the period around 10,500 BC. This differs by only 24 years from our rectified date of 10,476 BC for the onset of the full sunshine of the previous Golden Age—close enough to call a match.

This should make one sit up and take notice. In this chapter, the beginning and ending dates of the rectified cycle have been linked to a confluence of ancient prophetic traditions: Vedic, Christian, Judaic, Egyptian, and Mayan.

This illumines the ancient aphorism: "The Truth is only One, though the wise may speak about it differently."[14] For those who have pure intuition, all the varied expressions of truth, no matter how different in form they might appear, seem transparent and are understood in their true meaning.

# 4. HISTORICAL EVALUATION

## A New Historical Theoty

The rectified model of the cycle of ages allows us to calculate with some precision the periods and dates associated with both the beginning and end of the cycle as well as the ages themselves. This provides the basis for a new historical theory that demonstrates that the evolution of human consciousness and culture over the course of the last 13,000 years or so is tied directly to the declining cycle of the ages, in accordance with the views of the ancient sages.

The theory suggests that there is a deep dialectical process at work in human history, in which two opposing ideas, a thesis and antithesis, are integrated into a higher synthesis. The thesis posits that our individual lives unfold according to individual free will, reacting to chance and circumstance, while the antithesis counters that our collective life unfolds according to universal divine will, manifest by the influence of time. The theory takes both into account, demonstrating that human history is a synthesis of both influences simultaneously.

The thesis is familiar, for it is the perspective upon which most of modern historical thought is based. The antithesis is unfamiliar. Nevertheless it represents the perspective upon which most of ancient historical thought was based.

The ancients held that the evolution of human consciousness and culture follows a pattern, designed by the Creator, which unfolding over the course of thousands of years under *the influence of time,* makes manifest the will of God. This pattern is apparent in the sequence of four ages, called the Ages of Man, which unfold with clock-like precision from one cycle to the next.

Like all theories, the historical theory presented here is only as valid as its predictions. At this point, it has been shown that the rectified model provides predictions regarding the beginning and ending dates of the cycle, which are consistent with ancient prophetic thought. Now let us examine the sequence of ages and their intervening gaps in the light of both archeological and historical evidence.

## The Golden Age

The Vedic texts provide a clear window into the first age, the Golden Age, which dawned almost 13,000 years ago. The texts describe the period as one in which the *amritasya putrah*—the sons and daughters of immortality—wandered through the forests, subsisting on the natural bounty of Nature, and taking shelter beneath trees or in natural caves.

The texts go on to tell us that at that time there were no villages or cities, no forms of organized society. There were no class distinctions, such as kings, priests, merchants, and servants. There were no religions or religious rituals, and there were no material possessions to speak of. Even the institution of marriage did not exist. In other words, there was nothing whatsoever that might remind us of modern civilization or cultured society.

This is consistent with the proposed rectification scheme, which places the dawn of the previous Age of Truth in the tenth millennium BC—a period known in archeological circles as the Mesolithic, or Middle Stone Age.

The archeological evidence informs us that at that time there were no permanent cities or villages. Rather, the human population, far fewer in number than now, was organized into small family tribes that wandered over the face of the earth as hunter-gatherers, who took shelter beneath the trees, in makeshift dwellings, or in caves. In other words, it represents a pre-civilized era devoid of all the trappings of modern culture and civilization.

From our modern materialistic perspective, such a life hardly seems "golden" at all. But we are missing the point. The ancients looked back with nostalgia upon this period, not because it was a period of high material culture, but because it was a period of high spiritual culture, when our enlightened ancestors were lost in a state of divine contemplation and absorbed in the experience of God as they wandered through the forests and across the plains.

This characterized the age of natural innocence, before the corruptive influence of Ego infected the human soul. The souls that wandered the earth at that time were in a perpetual state of true surrender, and, like the lilies of the field, depended upon divine providence, rather than individual incentive, for their subsistence. They were not ignorant savages. They were illumined souls, who mingled with the gods and enjoyed a paradisical existence in a veritable Garden of Eden.

The coming Golden Age will resemble the previous in the sense that it, too, will be an age of natural innocence. But we will not go back to living in the forests and taking shelter beneath the trees or in caves. All the technological development achieved to date will be preserved, but transformed by a new and spiritual type of science, which will add great comfort and convenience to human life, while doing no harm to the environment and completely eliminating our struggle for survival.

Not only will humanity become enlightened *en masse;* our cultures, sciences, technologies, and life-styles will become enlightened as well. We are about to develop a civilization that will coexist peacefully with Nature and will serve to nourish the earth, rather than destroy it. As a result, we will be in paradise once again, but on a higher level of our evolutionary spiral.

## The Knowledge of Good and Evil

The rectified cycle suggests that around 6100 BC, the Golden Age, the age of natural innocence, ended and an intervening gap of about 380 years ensued, during which there was a transition to the second age. In this period a thin veil of ignorance descended over the human soul, and individual incentive, born of Ego, started to become manifest. Our ancestors had largely lost their natural innocence, replaced by the knowledge of good and evil.

In the Biblical myth of the Garden of Eden this transformation is symbolically represented by the "Fall," when the wily Serpent, the Ego, first tempted the human soul to partake of the knowledge of good and evil, something previously forbidden.

Our ancestors had been warned about this eventuality. Regarding the tree of the knowledge of good and evil, the Biblical myth has the Lord saying to Adam: "on the day that you eat from it, you will certainly die."[15]

However, the death that comes when the soul partakes of this forbidden knowledge is not physical; rather, it is spiritual. The soul dies to eternal life and obtains a mortal existence, where it must live under the tyranny of Ego.

This Fall from divine grace that affected our collective soul occurred some eight-thousand years ago, resulting in our banishment from paradise. Animal skins replaced fig leaves, and man-made dwellings replaced the forest. As a result, civilization was born.

## The Second Age of Seer-Kings

The proposed rectification scheme suggests that the second age spanned approximately 3,580 years, and lasted from around 5722-2142 BC.

The Vedic texts inform us that during this age the first royal dynasties, the first religious institutions, and the first sacred rituals were established. Again, this is consistent with the archeological evidence, which has established that during this lengthy period, the earliest known urban-spiritual civilizations, located in Egypt, Sumer, and India-Pakistan, emerged, developed, and eventually flourished.

During this second age, the majority of kings were righteous seer-kings, filled with the power of God, and the majority of priests were enlightened seer-priests, capable of cognizing eternal truth within their own awareness. As a result, the earliest known civilizations were largely spiritual civilizations, devoted to worshipping the gods and the pursuing the realization of spiritual immortality.

At this stage in our collective development, the veil of ignorance was thin and easily removed by those who regularly experienced the state of true surrender. As a result, many souls continued to experience the state of enlightenment. Such individuals were known as sages and seers, and the early societies looked to them for guidance and leadership.

However, these early societies were not completely immune to strife and war because the Ego had already emerged in collective society. But on the whole, they were peaceful societies, largely devoted to agriculture and various spiritual pursuits, including, especially in Egypt, the construction of large stone monuments and magnificent temples devoted to the gods.

## The Destruction of the Old Kingdoms

The 286-year gap that intervened between the second and third age took place between 2142-1856 BC. It was in this period that all three of the old spiritual kingdoms—the Vedic, the Egyptian and the Sumerian—were destined to fall apart. Eventually, new kingdoms, with more secular concerns and purposes, replaced the old kingdoms. But in the interim, during the gap, social chaos and turmoil prevailed.

The old spiritual kingdoms were all riverine cultures, the original Egyptian civilization being established along the Nile, the original Sumerian civilization, between the Tigris and Euphrates rivers in southern Iraq, and the original Indus-Sarasvati civilization, between the Indus and Sarasvati rivers in northwestern India and eastern Pakistan.

For reasons that are not clearly understood, the archeological record tells us that the original Egyptian civilization, known as the Old Kingdom, went into a period of social chaos starting around 2150 BC. For the next two-hundred years or so, the reins of power were divided among different groups and rapidly changed hands. Egyptologists commonly refer to this as the first intermediate period, which lies in between the Old Kingdom and what is called the Middle Kingdom.

It is also known that the original Sumerian civilization fell apart around the same time (2000 BC) due to an Akkadian invasion, which completely wiped out the Sumerian language and culture. In time, the conquerors adopted many of the old Sumerian ways, giving rise to a new Akkadian culture, similar in form. Later, this morphed into the Babylonian culture of Biblical fame.

In ancient India and Pakistan another important early civilization flourished. Referred to as the Indus-Sarasvati civilization, its many cities and villages were distributed along the banks of the Indus and the, now extinct, Sarasvati rivers.

Although not as widely known in the West Sumerian civilizations the size of the Indus-Sarasvati civilization exceeded that of the other two early civilizations combined, extending over an area roughly the size of Western Europe. It was equally ancient.

Like the other two, the Indus-Sarasvati civilization was also a seat of high culture and is credited with the earliest known examples of indoor plumbing. More significantly, in 1999, the earliest form of writing yet known was also found there, predating by some 200 years the Sumerian script, which previously held the record.

The archeological record indicates that the Indus-Sarasvati civilization also fell apart around 2000 BC. However, it appears that this was not due to internal social forces (as with the Egyptians) or external invasion (as with the Sumerians), but to a natural catastrophe.

Geological evidence suggests that around 2500 BC the ancient Sarasvati River, which was then a major river (several miles across at its mouth), flowing from the Himalayas to the Arabian Sea, began to dry up and by 1800 BC was nothing more than a dry riverbed.

As a result, the people in the area had to pick up and move further east to the Gangetic plains, where they resettled and built a new kingdom, which became the historical Vedic civilization.

We thus find that all three of the old kingdoms fell apart during the same period, corresponding to the 286-year gap between the second and third ages of the cycle. This provides additional evidence that our rectification scheme is accurate.

The causes responsible for the dissolution of the old societies were varied, but the results were the same. After an intermediate period of chaos and social confusion, a new age and social order began to take shape, which was driven by more secular forces. The second age of seer-kings was over and the third age of warrior-kings began.

## The Third Age of Warrior Kings

With the onset of the third age, the dark veil of ignorance became more firmly established in the human soul, and the leaders of society, which were previously enlightened, became infected by the corruptive influence of Ego.

As a result, unrighteous warrior kings, hell bent on conquest for the sake of wealth and power, began to emerge on the scene. The proposed rectification scheme suggests that third age lasted from 1856 BC to 529 AD. This marks a period that stretches from the emergence of Middle Kingdom Egypt to the fall of the Roman Empire, the last major empire of the ancient world.

During this period, human history is filled with the rise and fall of many different empires, accompanied by incessant warfare, bolstered by increasingly more powerful weapons of death and destruction. It also coincides with the emergence of many new religions, often married to the state in an enforced, unholy alliance.

During the age of warrior kings the plowshares of the people were hammered into swords, and the people were driven *en masse* to conquer other nations, often in the name of religion.

But the real motivating force behind the conquering armies was the lure of wealth and land, along with the acquisition of slaves. Ethical questions were thrown out the window in the bloodlust for wealth and dominion. As a result, the majority of the gods during this period appear as jealous or angry gods, who demanded vengeance and domination over others. All of this was due to the insidious influence of the Ego, which had even warped religions and wrapped the world and everything in it, in its tentacles.

The third age came to a close in December of 529 AD. In the following year, 530 AD, Justinian reconquered Europe, at which point the map of Europe was radically redrawn. This set the stage for the 200-year historical period known as the Dark Ages, when human civilization was once again thrown into a period of social chaos and turmoil, corresponding to another intervening gap.

## The Fourth Age of Spiritual Darkness

The rectification scheme suggests that the 191-year gap between the third and fourth ages took place between 529 AD and 720 AD, at which point the fourth age—the Age of Spiritual Darkness began.

The roughly 200-year period of social chaos that immediately followed the fall of the Roman Empire is well documented in the history books. During this period the ancient world dissolved in order to make way for the new modern world that was to come.

This was not a pleasant period. The organized society that flourished under the protection of the Roman Empire broke apart into small fiefdoms, or feudal states, often in conflict with one another, and all higher learning, especially all forms of classical learning, died out. For this reason it is called the Dark Age.

The historical Dark Age, which corresponds to the gap between the third and fourth ages, was followed by the onset of the fourth age, the Age of Spiritual Darkness, or Iron Age, when the dark veil of ignorance became as thick as night. This age was to last for almost 1200 years, until December 23, 1913, after which the final and most turbulent gap in the entire cycle ensued.

The Roman Catholic Church emerged as the dominant force from the fall of the Roman Empire, and played a pre-eminent role during the subsequent Age of Spiritual Darkness.

The Church effectively replaced the imperialistic aspect of the Roman Empire with religious fervor. In time the Roman Empire would be transformed into the Holy Roman Empire, which persisted until the time of Napoleon.

During the Renaissance, among the intelligentsia, the burgeoning awareness of Plato's writings and the Hermetic texts, created distaste for the rigid authoritarianism of the Church. Thinkers no longer wanted to be compelled and confined within narrow religious dogma, which had to be accepted solely on the basis of faith in Church authority. Intellectual circles began to seek the truth, outside, and regardless, of church dogma.

These circles, which were rebellious in their own time, gave rise to the impulse of free thought, which evolved, into the paradigm of modern objective science that sought to eliminate all subjectivity or religious strictures from the scientific investigation of nature. With Francis Bacon was born the doctrine of empirical science, based upon the inductive method of hypothesis and experimentation, replacing the subjective method of deduction and spiritual revelation.

In time this increasing momentum toward material, rather than spiritual, pursuits, gave rise to the industrial revolution of the nineteenth century, which accelerated the urbanization of society. With the advent of this revolution, various resources and materials became prime commodities, sought after by states and various business interests, and the banking industry, which controls the flow of money, situated itself as the ultimate controller of the destiny of nations—superceding even political control.

From the economic, political, and industrial scramble of the industrial revolution, the First World War was born. This took place in the first year of the final gap before the end of the cycle.

## The Final Countdown

The establishment of the Federal Reserve System not only marked the end of the fourth age, it also marked the beginning of the final gap—the final 95.5-year period that lies between the Age of Darkness and the coming Age of Truth. As predicted by the ancients, this period has proven to be the most deadly and tumultuous period in the history of the human race.

The First World War resulted in the loss of some 20-million lives. It was soon followed by the Great Depression, which in turn, was followed by the Second World War, resulting in the loss of another 60-million lives. The Second World War also brought us the Holocaust, involving mass genocide, and ended with the detonation of the first atomic bombs over Hiroshima and Nagasaki.

In Russia and China, the old orders were overthrown and replaced by communist regimes, with avowed atheist policies impacting billions of people. During communist rule in Russia it is estimated that at least 20-million people lost their lives in the work camps of frozen Siberia. No one knows how many millions died in the Chinese cultural revolutions of the 1960s, but the death and destruction did not end there. The Korean War, the Vietnamese War, the killing fields of Cambodia and Africa, and the constant revolutions in Central America all added millions more to the death toll.

It has been estimated that some 196-million people lost their lives either directly or indirectly due to wars waged over the twentieth century. This is more than the death toll from all previous wars fought during the long course of recorded history.

The signs thus suggest that we are currently in the final countdown of the long cycle of ages, which has defined the evolution of human culture and civilization over the course of the last 13,000 years. Whatever changes are coming, they are not likely to be trivial. The coming transformation may very well shake the foundations of modern civilization with unprecedented results.

## Summation

The archeological and historical evidence presented above provides direct support for the rectified cycle of four ages, including their intervening gaps. Looking back over the past, one can see that the model accurately predicts the most important changes in human consciousness, culture, and civilization that have taken place over the course of the last 13,000 years.

This should give increased confidence that the future prediction of the model will likely hold true as well. Of course, only time will tell, but if you have found the model convincing, it is advisable to make preparations now. The time is short and the potential cost of ignoring the predictions will be much more expensive than the potential cost of heeding them. Toward this end, during the remainder of this volume, we will discuss the practical preparations that might be of use.

# 5. PHYSICAL SURVIVAL

## A Global Food Crisis

To physically survive the coming seven-year period when we will be walking the straight and narrow path through the valley of the Shadow of Death, one must have enough food to eat and water to drink. Unfortunately, there is a global food crisis on the way.

The collapse of the US Treasury Bond Market and the subsequent collapse of the US dollar are inevitable. It is not a question of "if" these things will happen, it is only a question of "when." The rectified cycle of ages suggests that these things will happen sooner rather than later. In other words, there is not much time to prepare.

When these things occur, corporations will go bankrupt, dismiss their employees, and close their doors. At that time, the ships, trains, and trucks, which carry goods and commodities all around the world, will largely cease to operate. As a result the grocery shelves and the gas pumps will rapidly become empty. A black market in necessities will rapidly arise, making procurement difficult and expensive.

The farming industry, which is mostly run by large conglomerates, will also shut down. As a result, there won't be any food grown for the next season, unless produced by small family-owned farms. Even then, in the absence of gasoline or diesel, that food can't be delivered to market—even a local market—unless the farmer happens to own a horse-drawn cart. In a relatively short time, food will become a serious problem.

One might imagine that the governments will not allow this to happen. But here is an interesting fact. In May of 2007, the United States Department of Agriculture (USDA) released its projections of world grain supply and demand for the fiscal year 2007/2008. The projections were dismal.

The USDA projected that during this past year the global grain supply would fall to its lowest level in the forty-seven-year period that records have been kept. It also admitted that, except for the periods of First and Second World Wars, the grain supply would probably be lower than at any point in the last century—including the period known as the Great Depression.

In a press release issued at around the same time by the National Farmers Union the following announcement was made: "LOWEST FOOD SUPPLIES IN 50 OR 100 YEARS: GLOBAL FOOD CRISIS EMERGING." Among other things, the announcement stated:

> Most important, 2007/08 will mark the seventh year out of the past eight in which global grain production has fallen short of demand. This consistent shortfall has cut supplies in half-down from a 115-day supply in 1999/00 to the current level of 53 days.

In other words, in 2008 we had enough grain to feed the people of the world for only 53 days before the supply ran out—assuming no new grain was produced. This problem will be compounded by the even more dismal projections for the year 2008/2009.

The fact is that much of the world is currently locked in a major drought. The serious drought conditions in California and southwestern United States have been widely publicized. In the spring of 2009, an emergency was declared for agricultural sectors of California, because many of the crops in those areas were expected to fail due to lack of water. The southeastern portion of the United States is also experiencing drought conditions, though not as severe.

But this is only the tip of the iceberg. For the last few years Australia has been experiencing record drought conditions, which have reduced potential crops to withered stalks. The exceedingly dry conditions there have given rise to horrendous brush fires, destroying thousands of farms and homes.

The north-central region of China, which serves as the breadbasket for over one-billion people, has also been experiencing record drought conditions, resulting in an expected 40% shortfall of Chinese grain crops for this year. Major droughts are also underway in Africa and South America.

All of this adds up to an even more dramatic shortfall in grain supply for the current year as compared to last year, which was already the worst year on record. In all likelihood, the world grain stores will fall far below the 53-day supply by the summer of 2009.

I don't want to be an alarmist, but if you add to these problems an impending economic collapse then you have a recipe for disaster, and if you are not prepared then you will not survive. The government won't be able to help you.

Even if the governments of the world seized all existing grain supplies in order to fend off starvation, in the event of an economic collapse, the supplies won't last very long. If the farming operations shut down, because of financial failure, the supplies will soon run out, and mass starvation will ensue.

At the present time, the authorities don't want to raise additional concerns over food supplies, because they feel that there is already enough uncertainty in the world over economic conditions. But it would be foolish for us to stick our heads in the sand and ignore the situation, which is dire.

In the event of a sudden economic collapse, the impact of this global food shortage upon the people of the United States would be extreme. The problem is that most of the small farms in the United States have shut down. At the time of the Great Depression the vast majority of this country's population was rural, and many of those living in rural areas owned and operated small farms. As a result, families were able to feed themselves with home-grown crops.

Over the last eighty years, there has been an increasing urbanization of the US population, and a corresponding reduction in the number of small farms. In the 1970s farming subsidies were introduced, which mandated the United States government to pay farmers not to grow crops in an attempt to control commodity prices. As a result, even more small farms shut down.

Many small farmers sold off their equipment, stopped plowing their fields, and sat back to collect their farming subsidies—which paid them not to farm. Their children then grew up, went off to school, and took up residence in the cities, where they lost all knowledge of how to farm.

The truth is that the United States is not self-sufficient in its agricultural food production. Most of the farming operations today are run by large conglomerates, which tend to grow grains and soybeans for livestock and ethanol production, and not human consumption. As a result, the vast majority of domestic grain and food staples are imported from overseas.

In the event of a global economic collapse, and given the global food shortage that is already underway, do you think that foreign nations are going to send us their grain and food supplies, which they themselves are going to need to survive? Who will want to exchange their food supplies for dollars when the value of the dollar is rapidly declining, or when it becomes worthless? It doesn't take a genius to see that we will then find ourselves up the proverbial creek without a paddle.

If the farming conglomerates go bankrupt, the United States government may attempt to bolster domestic food production by enlisting people to work in federally-controlled farming cooperatives, where the workers receive food and shelter as their pay. But organizing such things will take time, and in the event of a sudden economic collapse, we won't have much time before the food runs out. The timeline is measured in days—not months or years.

It only takes four- to eight-weeks for a person to starve to death. How many United States citizens are prepared for such a catastrophe? How many do you think will survive? The answer is depressing. Yet this is not some far-fetched possibility—it is a very real possibility that is looming on the horizon.

Thus, my advice is to take steps now to prepare. Let your food stock be your insurance. If a food crisis doesn't develop, then you can always eat it, and no harm will be done. But if a food crisis does develop, and you have no food stock, then a great deal of harm will be done. It is better to be safe than sorry.

## A Global Energy Crisis

There is another serious problem that needs to be considered. If the coal mining and trucking corporations go bankrupt, dismiss their employees, and close their doors, then who will mine the coal required for our coal-fired electric power plants around the nation? Who will drive the trucks to deliver the coal? Without coal to fuel the generators, electricity will cease to flow through the wires.

A similar problem will arise in the heating oil industry. If the corporations that own the oil refineries go bankrupt, then who will produce the heating oil required to heat our homes? Who will drive the trucks to deliver the oil?

Even if the United States government steps in to take control of these industries, by conscripting a federal work force, as it is authorized to do in the case of a National Emergency, there will still be a shortage of both electricity and heating oil for the general population. These things are likely to be rationed out on a political basis in an attempt to maintain control over an increasingly unruly population.

How many people, who live in the northern half of the United States, will be able to survive the first winter following the economic collapse, without electricity or heating oil—a problem compounded by a severe shortage of food? Once again the answer is depressing.

It may seem unimaginable that our great country, whose cities and suburbs are filled with luxurious homes and well-stocked shopping malls, and whose roads are crammed with expensive automobiles and tractor-trailer trucks of all varieties, might be reduced to this deplorable state, where mere survival is the name of the game. But in spite of all appearances, we live in a very fragile society, and it is about to collapse. If we continue to hide our heads in the sand, and refuse to envision the worst-case scenarios, then we will be totally unprepared for catastrophe when it arrives.

If you live in a cold-climate, get yourself a wood-burning stove, or if that is not possible, then move to a warmer climate. It is better to avert the danger that has not yet come, than to suffer its consequences.

## Do Not Be Afraid

In his first inaugural address in 1933, made in the midst of the Great Depression, President Roosevelt uttered his famous statement:

> The only thing we have to fear is fear itself.

These words are even more applicable today, because we are about to face much more difficult times.

Over the course of the next few years there will be many things that might elicit fear in the human soul. Many will fear the loss of their possessions, the loss of their freedom, and even the loss of their lives.

But in truth there is nothing to fear at all—because you cannot be touched by any of these things. Speaking with absolute conviction born of direct spiritual experience, I can state categorically that you are immortal. You cannot die, even if your physical body is destroyed. The only thing you have to fear is fear itself, because in the final analysis none of these losses will affect you—the real you—in any way.

I realize that this understanding will provide little comfort to those facing such losses. But there is a kernel of wisdom here, which can be put into practical use.

During the process of transformation many things will arise that will readily inspire fear in the soul. My advice is do not give in to fear. Keep your hearts fixed on the goal and know that something good is happening, no matter how horrendous outward events and conditions may appear to be.

Do not succumb to fear, because that is precisely what the Ego wants. It wants us to remain in fear, so that we continue to fight demons of our own imagination rather than itself.

I am not advocating that we just give up and surrender ourselves to death and destruction. No, we must endeavor to survive. But we will have a much better chance of surviving if we do not succumb to fear. Whatever happens, we should keep our hearts fixed on the goal—the dawn of a new Age of Truth for all mankind—and adopt a neutral attitude to everything else.

If we succumb to fear, then our minds will become gripped by the evil that we imagine to be the source of that fear—and we will naturally want to destroy it. But by doing so, even if we think we are acting righteously, we will become aligned with the destructive forces that are under the control of the Ego—and that will only ensure our own destruction.

The ideal is to remain fearless and adopt an attitude of service. To maximize your own chance of survival, as well as those around you, become a nourisher—offer support and nourishment to your fellow human beings through acts of kindness and generosity, while keeping your heart fixed on the goal.

This will not guarantee your physical survival, but it will ensure your spiritual survival, for by behaving in this manner you will earn the keys to the Kingdom. If your actions are offered in service to others, while keeping your heart fixed on the goal, then your life will become the very embodiment of the Lord's Prayer:

> Thy kingdom come, thy will be done,
>
> On earth as it is in heaven.

The coming times of tribulation will test the patience and forbearance even of saints. Whether or not you wish to be counted among the saints is your choice, but we have arrived at the very threshold, prophesied in the Gospels when the meek shall inherit the earth.

# 6. SPIRITUAL SURVIVAL

## The Enemy Within

The root cause of the problems we are facing is not the system we have in place, nor the specific people in charge; it is the latent corruption in the human soul. Our true Enemy lies within, and it is called Ego.

The ancients were well aware of this Enemy and called it by name. In ancient Sanskrit the word for Ego was *ahamkara*—literally "I am the doer." The Ego represents that aspect of soul that leads the individual to believe that: "I am the thinker," "I am the doer," and "I am the perceiver." It is the source of all concepts of "me and mine" and "us versus them." In other words, it represents the "selfish" part of the human soul.

The Ego leads each of us to believe that "these are my thoughts, my actions, and my perceptions." Undoubtedly these statements may seem perfectly factual. But such beliefs are actually symptomatic of a deep-seated disease called Ego, which has infected the human soul for thousands of years. To regain paradise, to live in peace and harmony once again, this virulent and infectious disease must be eradicated.

The Ego is identified with everything it thinks, does, and perceives. It builds its identity from the thoughts of the mind, the actions of the body, and the perceptions of the senses. Just as any mother will fight to protect her offspring, so too, will the Ego fight to protect its self-constructed identity.

The Ego is driven to possess and control whatever it experiences, striving desperately to become the master of its own destiny and the creator of its own identity. Its lust for possessions and power is insatiable. No matter how many possessions it acquires, nor how much power it wields, it always wants more.

The reason for this, though simple, is not obviously apparent. Indeed, it is a hard-won spiritual insight. The Ego, by itself, has no real identity. In very truth, it is a non-identity—a mere absence of identity. As such, it hungers insatiably for identity. In an attempt to assuage its hunger, it is constantly busy with constructing and reinforcing a false identity for itself by accumulating experience, possessions, and power, which it claims as its own. These accumulated things feed the Ego, and the more it accumulates, the more insatiable it becomes.

But no matter how strong the Ego becomes, no matter how much wealth and power it acquires, it remains deeply insecure, because it is engaged in a fundamental act of deception. The Ego deceives the soul by providing it with a false identity, which is nothing more than a disguise to hide the fact that the Ego has no identity.

This deep-seated insecurity makes the Ego quick to feel threatened. Suspicious and hyper-vigilant, it is always on the lookout for anyone or anything that might diminish its pride in its power and possessions, thus threatening its fragile existence.

Also, despite appearance to the contrary, the Ego abhors competition. However, the Ego always wants to win and, unchecked by conscience or fear of moral censure, it may feel justified in using any means at its disposal to win. This includes ruthlessly eliminating its competition. The Ego is quick to label its competition as the enemy. This holds true on both individual and collective levels.

Once the competition becomes identified as the enemy, the Ego starts to dehumanize and stigmatize it as evil, because it is perceived as threatening its very existence.

Generally speaking, anything that supports and nourishes the existence of the Ego is deemed "good," while anything that threatens to diminish or destroy its existence is deemed "evil." This characterization allows the Ego to adopt a moral stance of righteous indignation as it seeks to crush its evil competition—in the name of all that is good.

Even religions are not immune to this corrosive influence. In the Bible, when Joshua led the Israelites into Canaan, they engaged in a war of extermination in the name of "their" God, and proceeded to slaughter every man, woman, and child in the villages they found there. During the tenth and twelfth centuries AD, when the followers of Mohammed invaded India, they sought to stamp out all competition to "their" God by beheading those who would not convert. When the Roman Catholic hierarchy, in the Middle Ages, organized the Albigensian crusade in southern France, they sought to stamp out all competition to "their" God by ruthlessly slaughtering hundreds of thousands of peaceful men, women, and children, often burning them at the stake for heresy.

Yet all of these atrocities were conducted for the sake of what was deemed "good"—even in the very name of God. This is the work of the Ego and not of God. In effect, the Ego has usurped the place of God; it has usurped the place of the true Self, and its tentacles now hold the entire world in its deadly embrace.

It would be a mistake for any one of us to imagine that we are immune to this influence. Not one of us is immune. It is latent in every person that conceives the world in terms of me and mine, or us and them.

The Ego may operate more unchecked in some souls than in others, but given the right circumstances, it could rear its ugly head in any of us. Its deceptions have the potential to convince the naïve and fearful soul that it is right and necessary to commit atrocities, to destroy life and property, to enslave others, or to appropriate their wealth. These things may be deemed acceptable because the Ego is skilled in justifying such acts, by convincing the soul that they have to be performed in the name of what is good—in the name of survival.

It is the existence of the Ego, our age-old Enemy within, that gives truth to the notion that "power tends to corrupt, and absolute power corrupts absolutely." Given the potential for the Ego to corrupt the soul, there is simply no escape from this conclusion.

## The Monster in the Basement

The key to spiritual survival involves learning how to eliminate the Ego, which can be compared to a monster in the basement. Let me develop this analogy by using a somewhat childlike parable.

One upon a time there was a person who lived in a pleasant, light-filled house, with a deep dark basement. In this parable, the house represents the mind-body complex and the person represents the soul that dwells therein. The ordinary activities that take place in the house can then be compared to the ordinary activities of the mind and body—which take place on the surface levels of thought, action, and perception.

Like most of us, this person genuinely wanted to create a happy home and was industrious in trying to do so. He busied himself with cooking, cleaning, and entertaining friends. But his constant activity was prompted by a hidden motivation. He had to stay busy to keep himself distracted from his deepest fear—that a monster lived in his basement. To keep his sanity, he felt that he had to ignore the monster and avoid the basement at all costs.

Here, the steps leading down to the basement represent the sub-conscious levels of the mind, which are hidden beneath the surface, while the basement represents the very basis of the mind, which is hidden behind a closed door.

He could sense the ominous influence of this monster, because from time to time, and especially at night, it made horrible noises, and an eerie glow shone through the cracks in the basement door, which terrified him.

At night, when he suspected that the monster emerged from the basement to haunt the house, he would dive beneath the covers of his bed, where he shivered in fear, leaving the monster to have its way with all the things in the house. But then the new day dawned and things seem okay, because the monster had retreated back into the basement. In this manner, he learned to live with the monster, while trying to maintain a happy home.

But then one day, he awoke to find that the monster, during the course of the previous night, had wreaked havoc with the house. Everything was out of order: the contents of drawers were on the floor, the furniture was in disarray, and the house was covered in slime and filth.

This was too much for the owner of the house. He just couldn't live this way anymore. He realized that in spite of all his efforts to live happily, the monster was actually ruining his life, and he knew that it would destroy him if he continued to ignore it. But he didn't want to leave his house. So what was he to do?

He decided that to live a normal life and have a happy home, he must confront his greatest fear. He must confront the monster in the basement and destroy it once and for all. Imagining the monster to be both hideous and powerful, the very embodiment of the Devil himself, this was a terrifying prospect, and he had no idea how to defeat it.

Nevertheless, having no choice, he mustered his courage, and began to venture down the dark stairs. With every descending step, the monster became more agitated, howling and moaning, while emitting eerie flashes of light from behind the closed door. Terrified, the man longed to turn back, but knew that he must persist if he were ever to free himself from the demon.

Finally he reached the door and as he gingerly touched it, all hell broke loose. The house started to shudder and tremble and a thunderous roar was heard, as if the whole world were under the power of the demon behind the door. Then, steeling himself, he flung the door open and stepped inside.

To his amazement, he found that the room was empty. No one was home—nothing was there. The instant he opened the door and stepped inside, all the terrible sounds and shaking suddenly stopped. All that remained was a dark and empty room, silent as a tomb.

Relieved, yet mystified, he could come to no other conclusion than that the whole thing was just his imagination. There was no monster in the basement. In truth it did not exist, because in reality the Ego is a big fraud—a non-entity. All that exists in the basement is a dark and empty room.

From that time forward, the owner lived a truly happy life. Whenever he heard sounds coming from the basement, all he had to do was descend the steps and open the basement door. He had only to step inside for all the noises to stop. At that point, he became free from fear. The monster in the basement had been banished into nothingness.

## Know thy Enemy

The above parable reveals both the true nature of the Ego and how to banish it. The words of Sun Tzu, who wrote the Art of War, an ancient Taoist treatise still used by military and business strategists around the world, offers valuable wisdom with respect to this inner struggle:

> If you know your Enemy and know your Self, you will not be imperiled in a hundred battles; if you do not know your Enemy but do know your Self, you will win one and lose one; if you do not know your Enemy nor your Self, you will be imperiled in every single battle.

This illumines our problem: We lack knowledge. We neither know our true Enemy, nor do we know our true Self. As a result, we are imperiled in every battle and must live in constant fear.

Because of our ignorance, we are in a state of constant war with ourselves. Yet all our enemies are imaginary. Our true Enemy lies within our own mind and not outside in the environment.

We imagine our enemies to be another person, another nation, another army, another corporation, or another religion. But our true Enemy lies within, at the very basis of our minds, and if we are ever to defeat it we must confront it and come to know it—as it is in itself. In this regard, Sun Tzu gives another piece of sage advice:

> To know your Enemy, you must become your Enemy.

This is a mysterious statement, no doubt. So what does it mean? It means that if we are to know the Ego, we must become the Ego. It means that we must descend into the darkness of our own subconscious, open the door to the basement of the mind, and step inside. We must immerse ourselves in the silent darkness, the emptiness, which represents the true nature of the Ego.

The Ego can be imagined as an inhabitant in the basement. But in actuality, all that exists in the basement is a dark and empty room. When we descend the stairs and step inside that room, we inhabit it. At that point, we become the inhabitant in the basement. In other words, we become the Ego.

Only then do we come to know what the Ego really is—a non- entity—a mere absence of identity. One might imagine that this absence is the Self, but it is not. Rather, this absence is the non-Self—the Ego—the Enemy of the Self.

To realize the true nature of the Ego, we must transcend the process of thinking, and go beyond "the knowledge of good and evil." We must follow a thought to its source—at the very basis of the mind. This can be compared to descending the dark stairs that lead to the basement. Upon reaching the last step—the finest and deepest level of the thinking process—we must then transcend thought altogether. This can be compared to opening the basement door.

Then we will discover that there is nothing there. There is nothing at the basis of the mind but silent and empty darkness. That is the true nature of the Ego. It is but a veil of silent darkness, a veil of emptiness, whose nature is to cover, hide, or obscure the true nature of the Self.

This veil can also be described as a veil of pure ignorance, for when the soul enters the silent darkness, by transcending thought, it ignores everything. It forgets or ignores all things in this world or any other world.

Just as darkness is not anything positive, but just an absence of light, so also, ignorance is an absence of knowledge. The irony is that to know the Ego, as it is in itself, one must come to know nothing—for the Ego is sheer nothingness.

That is what we must become if we are to know our Enemy. We must become a non-entity, a being that has no identity, a nameless soul without a form. We must become the nameless, formless inhabitant in the basement. But that is not our true Self.

## Know thy Self

Above the entrance to Plato's academy a famous injunction was inscribed, which read: "Know Thy Self." This is the second part of the problem: we do not know our Self. According to Sun Tzu, knowing our Enemy is not sufficient. To become truly free from peril, we must also know our Self

The difficulty is that the Ego hides the Self, covering it with a veil of silent empty darkness. Lifting that veil is the true Apocalypse: the Final Event of every mortal soul. Only then can we know the true Self—the immortal Self, which is the same in all beings. In that instant, mortality vanishes and immortality is born. The Ego is slain, and the true Self shines forth. That is the true victory alluded to in the previously cited quote from *First Corinthians:*

But how does one lift the veil, escape the ignorance, or remove the darkness? When the soul becomes one with the silent darkness, it is incapable of doing anything— thinking, speaking, acting, or perceiving. As a result, there is nothing whatsoever that the soul can "do" to remove the darkness.

In that state, all the soul can do is to "do nothing," Like a babe in the womb or a corpse in the tomb, all it can do is wait for its delivery. When the soul reaches the thoughtless state at the basis of the mind, it has reached the alpha and omega of its mortal existence. It is incapable of going any further on its own volition. The only thing it can do is to "surrender"—to stop trying to do anything.

It is only when the soul is in the thoughtless state—the state of true surrender—that the switch can be flipped and the light turned on. But it is not the mortal soul who turns it on; rather it is turned on by the immortal Self, the same in all beings. That immortal Self can also be understood as a ray of God, the Supreme Being. In other words, the Self illumines itself, by itself, through itself alone—spontaneously and naturally—without any effort on the part of the individual soul.

Like a Divine Fisherman, the immortal Self fishes souls from the sea of Death and carries them to the shore of eternal Life. This is true salvation. But the Self can only save those who have given up trying to swim, who have surrendered everything, including the act of thinking, to God, the Supreme Being, who in the final analysis is the Supreme Self of all.

As long as the Ego is active, as long as its corrosive influence pervades our minds and bodies, we cannot be saved. In order to be saved, we must first banish the Ego, the great Satan, to the Pit. We must banish the beast to its dark lair, the basement at the bottom of the mind, and hold it there, by remaining there ourselves—without any thought of this world or the next—like a corpse in a tomb. Only then, can we be resurrected from the Dead and delivered like a babe unto eternal Life.

When this occurs, and it happens in an instant, in the twinkling of an eye, the veil of darkness is removed by the Light, which destroys ignorance. It is removed by Fullness, which replaces Emptiness. In that instant, one comes to know the Self, which lies beyond all darkness, ignorance, and emptiness.

From that moment forward, one becomes untouchable by Death. The soul obtains its true Identity, which cannot be threatened by anything within the created universe. The mind might stop functioning and the body might die, but the Self is immortal. It lives on forever and has no dependence upon the mind or body.

As a result, when one comes to know the Self, all perils vanish and one becomes fearless. For such an enlightened soul, all enemies are disarmed. The Self is always a friend to the Self, and it sees the Self in all. Upon realizing the Self, one is rendered fearless and a friend to everything that exists, eternally free from the corrupting influence of Ego. This is the ultimate destiny of every living soul, and to fulfill that destiny we have only to do—NOTHING.

## The Great Humbling

Over the course of the next few years there will be a tremendous loss of ownership, wealth, and power, both individually and collectively. I call this the "Great Humbling," because these conditions will cause the Ego to be humbled and brought to its knees.

Through this Great Humbling, the human race will come to realize that it is not the master of its own destiny, and that our egos have led us astray into the abyss of self-destruction. Each of us will then be given a great opportunity—the opportunity to banish the Ego and reduce it to nothingness.

## A Three-Stage Process

To finally rid ourselves of the collective Ego, our age-old Enemy, a three-stage process is required. The first stage involves the Great Humbling, which will weaken the Ego, rendering it vulnerable.

The second stage involves banishing the Ego to the Pit, that is, to the basement at the bottom of the mind, by transcending the process of thinking and experiencing the fact that the basement is empty: "no one is home."

The third stage involves taking up residence in the basement, at which point the Ego will become utterly incapable of rearing its ugly head. This is the stage of surrender. One must learn how to remain in the silent darkness that exists at the basis of the mind, without attempting to think or do anything.

This is the "Dark Night of the Soul" spoken of by the great saints in many traditions—the darkest hour before the dawn. The dawn will come of its own accord. In time the veil of darkness will be removed, the light of the Self will shine forth, and the Ego will be slain. For that you don't need to do anything. You merely have to do NOTHING.

The Great Humbling is going to happen whether we like it or not. It is going to happen automatically through the influence of time.

Similarly, the third stage is also automatic. There is nothing that we need to do to bring it about. We merely have to do NOTHING. The Ego will be slain for you. It will be slain by the light of the Self—the light of God, which will shine through the influence of time.

The only stage that requires us to do anything of significance is the second stage. To banish the Ego to the Pit, we have to descend the dark steps that lead to the basement at the bottom of the mind, open the closed door, and step into the room. But this is not as hard as it sounds. In what follows I offer some practical advice that will make the whole process simple, easy, and natural.

## The Ancient Technique of Meditation

In order to banish the Ego to the Pit, we need a strategy, a plan of action. The ancients came up with such a strategy long ago, which they put into widespread practice. This strategy involves a simple mental technique, which employs the mind and senses—a technique called meditation.

A 'technique' can be understood as a methodology that allows one to accomplish something that might otherwise be challenging while minimizing the effort. All such techniques are based upon fundamental laws of nature.

For example, the technique of leverage utilizes a lever to move heavy objects by taking advantage of the law of proportion. Similarly, the technique of irrigation involves creating channels to draw in water from a river or lake to irrigate a field by taking advantage of the law of gravity.

The ancients, faced with the same age-old Enemy as we are today, sought a technique, based upon general laws of nature, which would enable them to banish the Ego with minimum effort and without fear. They found these laws in the operation and nature of the mind.

By simple observation, they discovered a fundamental truth. Just as water has a natural tendency to flow downhill, so also, the mind has a natural tendency to seek fields of greater satisfaction, charm, and interest.

This is part of our everyday experience. How many times have you been in a crowded room, engaged in some boring conversation, while your mind is flitting around the room until it alights on some more interesting conversation overheard in the background? The person in front of you might continue talking, but you are no longer paying attention. Your mind has gone elsewhere, to a field of greater satisfaction, charm, and interest. Moreover, it has moved on spontaneously, without any effort on your part.

This not only applies to interesting conversations, it also applies to sensory perceptions. The mind is naturally attracted to things of beauty and charm. If you walk into a crowded room, your attention will automatically be drawn to the most attractive and charming person in the room. This might be an infant, a young child, a beautiful woman, or a handsome man. It will be whatever the mind finds most attractive and charming.

Even if you try to fight this natural attraction, you will still find yourself stealing furtive glances in the direction of the charismatic person. This is a fundamental law of nature—a law of attraction—which the mind spontaneously obeys. This law was the first discovery of the ancients, which pertains to the operation of the mind.

The second discovery pertains to the very nature of the mind. To use a simple analogy, the mind can be compared to a pond. In this analogy, one's thoughts can be compared to bubbles rising from the bottom of the pond to burst on the surface. This is where we normally grasp our thoughts—on the surface level of the thinking mind.

The ancients discovered that there are deeper levels of thinking, hidden below the surface. The thoughts experienced on these deeper levels can be compared to bubbles rising from the bottom of the pond, before they burst on the surface.

They then discovered something very fundamental about the nature of the mind—that these deeper levels of thinking are far more satisfying, interesting, and charming than those experienced on the surface. This might seem counterintuitive, especially given the alternate analogy, which compares the process of experiencing deeper levels of thinking to descending dark steps leading to the basement, but it is actually quite true.

The deeper levels of thinking are more expansive, subtle, and abstract, as well as less defined. If the surface level of thinking is compared to shouting, then the deeper levels of thinking can be compared to whispering. When a person whispers, we naturally lean in to hear what is being said. In the same manner, when given a chance, the mind naturally leans into the subtler and quieter levels of thinking.

Because these deeper levels of thinking are more expansive and less defined, the mind finds great freedom there. They are innately satisfying to the mind, which craves freedom from the prison, imposed upon it by the Ego.

Because these deeper levels are subtler, the mind finds great charm there as well. Subtle thoughts are nuanced in a way that cannot be grasped on the more concrete surface level of thinking. This makes them more intriguing and charming.

Due to the natural tendency of the mind to seek fields of greater satisfaction, charm, and interest, once introduced to the process of meditation, the mind naturally and spontaneously goes within to experience these deeper levels of thought. The key is that we have to give it a chance to do so.

This is where the Great Humbling comes into play. The Ego is a slave driver, desirous of keeping the mind under its control, and constantly directing the mind toward the outer world of experience to gather possessions, wealth, and power that it can use to further reinforce its false identity and consolidate its control.

Under these conditions, the mind rarely gets a chance to settle down and go within. Low or high levels of anxiety and stress, cravings for enjoyment and achievement, all keep it highly active and outwardly directed. But this is counter-productive to what we want to achieve.

When we begin to experience the Great Humbling, the outer world will become much less attractive, filled with the experience of loss and uncertainty. These conditions will be highly distasteful to the Ego, and as a result, it will stop pushing the mind in an outward direction so insistently. This will be our opportunity to close our eyes and go within.

Granted there may be various responsibilities or objectives that might inhibit you from going within. You may, for example, be trying to nourish and support those in your environment, by caring for the sick, or providing food and water for your family and others. In such cases, you must, of course, tend to what is necessary. But do not forget the great opportunity to banish the Ego and nourish the Self. Care for yourself by making time to go within.

If you have decided to fight and are plotting against outer enemies, consider that you may be making the wrong choice. In doing so, it will be much more difficult for you to find the time and peace to go within. This is a warning sign that if you don't change your ways, you will be lost.

Let us assume you have made the right choice, and that from time to time, when not performing service to others, you are given the chance to close your eyes and go within. What then?

## Find Time to Meditate

Make finding time to meditate a discipline. If you are performing service to others and feel that you cannot spare the time to close the eyes and go within, then you are under the control of the Ego.

No amount of "good works" will save you. The only thing that will save your soul is absolute surrender to the thoughtless state, which involves doing NOTHING—no good works at all.

So, learn to balance the amount of time you spend in service with the amount of time you spend in meditation. Service to others is a good thing and should not be abandoned. But if you spend all your time doing that, and don't take time to meditate, then even though you may save the lives of others, you will be committing spiritual suicide against your Self.

Lets assume that you find the time to close the eyes with the intention to meditate. What are you supposed to do?

## Choose an Object of Meditation

Ideally, one should learn how to meditate from an instructor, who has been trained in the ancient practice.[16] Personal instruction, conveyed by word of mouth, is always superior to written instruction read in a book. Meditation has been taught this way for thousands of years.

However, the urgency of the time and your current situation may preclude this possibility. If you are going to teach yourself how to meditate by following the instructions in this book then the first thing you need to do is to choose an object of meditation. This will be the thought that you follow within.

In India a *mantra* may be supplied by a teacher. This is simply a sacred sound imparted to one verbally, which is to be repeated mentally, without moving one's tongue or lips.

The use of a sound or mantra as the object of meditation is probably the easiest way to transcend. For example, you might choose the name of your chosen deity, or a short phrase from a familiar prayer, as the object of meditation. Either would serve just fine. You could also use a sacred image, such as an icon or symbol. In either case, the sound or image is to be entertained mentally, on the level of thinking, with the eyes closed.

Staring at a candle flame or a divine image, reciting some passage from scripture, or even saying a prayer, is a waste of time when it comes to transcending. All of these things will keep the mind occupied on the surface level of thinking and will be counter productive to the process.

If you are choosing the object for yourself, then you will be safe in choosing the name or image of the God of your religious tradition. From this point forward I am simply going to refer to the object of meditation, whatever it might be, as the mantra.

## Initiating the Practice

Before beginning the process of meditation choose a comfortable place to sit, preferably free from distractions, such as the quiet solitude of your own room. Obviously a windy place, or a place where you are exposed to biting insects, is not ideal.

You should sit up during meditation. Lying down will have a tendency to dispose you to sleep due to habit. It is not necessary to sit up erect in the lotus position. You can sit in a comfortable chair, or on your bed with pillows propped up behind your back, but a sitting position is definitely preferable to a reclining one.

Once seated, it would be helpful to take a few deep slow breaths through your nostrils. This will help calm the mind and free it from previous distractions. Then simply close your eyes, wait about thirty seconds to calm the mind even further, and then introduce the mantra as a faint mental idea and then, most importantly, let the mantra go.

Introduce the thought of the mantra easily and effortlessly, without trying to concentrate upon it and without trying to hold onto it. Your job is simply to introduce the idea. Then let it go.

The purpose of meditation is not to "think about" the mantra in terms of its meaning. If you are using a name or image of God, it doesn't help you at all to think about the glory of God or God's attributes. That is called contemplation, and though contemplation may be useful, it is not helpful for the purpose of meditation because it keeps the mind active on the conscious level of thinking.

When you let go of the mantra, it may change. The sound might get softer or quieter, the image might become less distinct or more hazy, etc. That's fine. Don't try to bring the mantra into sharp focus. That is called concentration, and that too is unhelpful to the process of meditation.

By concentrating upon the thought of the mantra, you are effectively holding onto it. That will disallow the mind from sinking deeper to experience the thought on subtler and more abstract levels of the thinking process.

Do not try to concentrate on the mantra, or to control it in any way. Simply introduce the thought or idea of the mantra and let go of it. That's all there is to it. Initiating the practice is simple and easy. It is as natural as thinking a thought.

## Take it Easy

At some point, you will forget about the mantra. That's natural and expected. Just initiate the process again, as you did before, and generally just take it easy. This is not meant to be hard work. You don't have to try to make it happen. The key word is innocence. Let the process happen by itself.

You can think of the process as diving into a pond. When you introduce the mantra and let it go, the mind naturally begins to dive within. This is called the inward stroke of meditation.

When you lose the mantra, the mind naturally resurfaces, by riding up on the bubbles of other thoughts. That is supposed to happen. It is part of the process of purification and is called the outward stroke of meditation.

So the process of meditation involves both an inward and an outward stroke. All we have to do is initiate the process by introducing the mantra. That begins the inward stroke. Everything else happens automatically. The mind resurfaces on its own.

Each time you lose the mantra, each time the mind floats up to the surface by means of other thoughts—know that something good is happening. The latent impressions in the mind are being cleared out. That is the natural result of the inward stroke. It serves to flush out the latent impressions of the mind—i.e., all the useless stuff stored in the mind and hoarded by the Ego.

When you are getting rid of the garbage in your house, you simply take it outside for the garbage man. You don't need to sift through the bag of garbage to get rid of it. In the same way, it serves no purpose to analyze the thoughts that come up during meditation. That would be like sifting through the garbage.

Just know that something good is happening, and when you realize that you are no longer thinking the mantra, come back to it, as easily and effortlessly as you think any other thought. That will initiate the next inward stroke.

Do not try to block out other thoughts. Neither engage them, nor avoid them. Have a neutral attitude to all other thoughts in meditation—whatever they might be. Some of them might be quite pleasant, others might be quite unpleasant. It doesn't matter. They are all garbage.

You might have a brilliant idea in meditation—a stroke of genius, a solution to a long-standing problem. Fine. But deal with it after you have finished your meditation. As far as the process of meditation is concerned, it is still garbage.

When the mind has been cleaned out through regular practice, then upon introducing the mantra and letting it go, the mind will immediately sink within and transcend the process of thinking altogether. That is characteristic of a clean, healthy and innocent mind, in its natural and pristine state. As long as the inward stroke is still flushing out the garbage, you still need to meditate.

Each meditation is like taking a mental bath. It serves to cleanse the mind over time. The mind is filled with lifetimes of dirt and grime, stored in the form of mental impressions, so don't expect to come out absolutely clean after your first meditation.

After each meditation you will come out cleaner, and your mind will begin to behave in a more innocent manner, freer from the corruptive influence of ego—but don't expect to be absolute free and clear after your first meditation.

It doesn't matter how long it takes to fully cleanse and heal the mind. The important thing is that you have begun the process. You are on the correct path and moving in the right direction, rather than just wandering around aimlessly accumulating more and more garbage. With each meditation you will lighten your load.

It may happen, and often does, that the idea of the mantra is there along with other thoughts at the same time. That, too, is okay. Just have a neutral attitude toward the other thoughts and favor the mantra—without trying to cling to it.

Sometimes the mind might be filled with tons of chattering thoughts in competition with each other and with the mantra. Just take it easy and know that something good is happening. The mind is boiling over and dumping out a lot of garbage. Don't get upset. Just favor the mantra when you can, and let the mind do its thing.

This might happen for an entire meditation, or it might happen every time you meditate over the course of several days. Don't imagine that you have failed, or that you are incapable of meditating. I have been there and know how frustrating it can be to have an erratic and frenetic mind that just won't seem to settle down. But it is all part of the process. When the garbage has been cleared out, then the mind will be that much cleaner and that much more capable of diving within without such distractions.

To reiterate, the process of meditation is two-fold: (i) it starts with an inward stroke designed to enable the mind to fathom deeper levels of the thinking process and then transcend the process of thinking altogether, and (ii) this results in an outward stroke, which serves to clear out obstacles that might prevent the process of transcending from taking place.

You won't be able to achieve (i) in any permanent manner unless and until you have gone through the process of (ii). You can't have a clean house, unless you take the time to clean it. It is that simple. The cleaning process is not hard. It just takes time.

## The Great River of Time

Fortunately, at this special juncture, the influence of time is on our side. In the past it has been difficult for people to meditate, because of the strength of the Ego, which will do everything it can to distract one from going within. This is the monster in the basement trying to scare you or lure you away from discovering your true Self.

With the Great Humbling, our collective Ego will become weakened and the earth itself—the planetary being will begin its own global meditation.

During the next forty-two months there will be a strong undertow in the minds of all, pulling us within on a global inward stroke and the garbage is going to be flying out all over the place. This will be the time to unload "all" of your garbage through the help and assistance of the planetary being, who, in turn, is being assisted by the Supreme Being.

One beautiful thing about the mind is that when it unloads its garbage, it doesn't pollute the environment. The garbage just dissipates like a dream in the night. It gets swallowed up by the Absolute and ceases to exist.

But if you don't take the time to sit quietly with the eyes closed and thus allow the process of meditation to take place; if you keep yourself active all the time in an attempt to fight against your imagined enemies, or even to serve your friends, you will be swimming against the current—in effect, you will be fighting against the will of God.

All the denizens of heaven will be on our side as we engage in meditation over the coming few years, and what may have taken many years or lifetimes to achieve before, will be accomplished very quickly. A great flowing river is about to open up in the minds of all. Let it do the work and carry you to the goal.

In this regard, consider the story of Hercules. He was assigned the enormous task of cleaning out the stables of the gods. This is another parable, in which the horses of the gods represent the senses, and the stables of the gods represents the mind, the home of the senses, and the place where all the excretions of the senses are stored.

Upon being assigned the task, Hercules quickly realized that it was almost impossible. It would take him thousands of years to clean out all the filth in the stables. But then he had a brilliant idea. He would let Nature do all the work for him.

He simply diverted a nearby river to flow through the stables, and in a short time all the filth was washed away by the flowing water, with hardly any effort on his part at all. That is precisely what is about to happen.

The great river of the Divine Mind—the purifying influence of time—will soon be flowing through all of our individual minds. It will quickly clear out all the filth and garbage that we have stored up inside, and if we surrender ourselves to its current, it will take us to the goal. We simply have to stop fighting the current.

In short, the next few years will mark the most auspicious time to meditate in the last 52,000 years. That is why there are close to seven billion people on our planet. Everyone has come to take advantage of the opportunity, whether they are conscious of it or not.

Even though it may be a turbulent ride at the outset, do your best not to miss the boat. You won't be sorry. We are about to set sail for the other shore—the shore of Eternal Life, which lies far beyond the sea of Death.

## Knowledge and Ignorance

The soul that exists in the thoughtless state is faced with a perplexing situation. In order to obtain final liberation, it must first cross over the sea of Death. It must remove the veil of pure ignorance that hides its own immortal Self. But the soul itself is incapable of doing this. All it can do is remain in the silent darkness, in a thoughtless state of pure ignorance, waiting for its delivery. The Vedic sages summed up this perplexing situation with the following statement:

> Knowledge and ignorance—whoever knows these two together, crosses over Death by means of ignorance, and attains Eternal Life by means of knowledge.[17]

The statement holds the key to final liberation. It tells us how to cross the sea of Death. This is accomplished by doing

NOTHING—by simply remaining in pure ignorance, without any thought of this world or the next. In that state of true surrender, the soul will be carried across the sea of Death by the grace of God.

The soul established in the state of pure ignorance has no way to initiate or facilitate this crossing, because it is incapable of thinking or doing anything. All it can do is to wait like a babe in the womb for its delivery.

Upon arriving at the other shore, the soul obtains gnosis— pure and direct cognition of the Divine. Although the soul crosses over Death by means of pure ignorance, it attains Eternal Life by means of pure knowledge.

With this attainment, one realizes the immortal Self after the Ego is slain. That is true victory over Death. That is our collective destiny, and that alone will ultimately usher in a new Golden Age, a new Age of Truth for all mankind.

# 7. A VISION OF THE COMING AGE

## The Age of Truth

We now stand at the most important juncture in time that has ever been experienced by human beings on earth. We are about to witness the dawn of a new Golden Age, or Age of Truth, as well as the dawn of a new epochal day for all humanity.

The coming Age of Truth will not be identical to the previous, which took place some 13,000 years ago. We will not move back into the forests to live in caves, but we will come to live in a new-found paradise, where the human soul is fully in tune with Nature and at peace with itself once again. This is the Redemption of Man spoken of by the scriptures.

We will not abandon technology or science. Rather, we will transform our technology and science to reflect spiritual truth. Instead of serving to destroy Nature, our technologies will serve to nourish it. Rather than being enslaved to our possessions, our possessions will serve us in our quest to create heaven on earth.

A whole new type of science and technology will emerge based upon the imperishable structure of pure knowledge that resides within the Self. This will be a science of consciousness that will make our current physical sciences seem like primitive theories of undeveloped minds. On the basis of this new science, wonderful new technologies will be developed that provide convenience and leisure to the human population, while simultaneously nourishing our souls and the soul of Nature.

In times to come we will develop into true citizens of the universe, capable of exploring the vast realms of the Cosmos, both spiritually and technologically. Our awareness will extend far beyond the small confines of this planet into the vastness of the starry heavens, and there we will find brothers and sisters from whom we have been separated for too long.

War and poverty will become a thing of the past and the earth will blossom with new species of plants and animals, not born of genetic engineering, but of the will of God. We will know how to act as their compassionate caretakers. As in days of old, we will tend the trees in our new Garden in accordance with the will of God, and for many thousands of years to come, no one will be tempted by the wily Serpent to taste of the tree of the knowledge of good and evil—for we will treasure the recovery of the Tree of Life.

Once again we may be known as the *amritasya putrah*, the sons and daughters of immortality, and we will eventually ascend the stairway to the sky to obtain full immortality in the bosom of the infinite, for that is our highest destiny. There we will merge with the Lord of Immortality—the inconceivable reality of the Supreme Being, who has no beginning and no end.

## The Ideology of Social Holism

As the Age of Truth unfolds a new type of society will be established on earth, which will be unlike anything known in recorded history. Generally speaking, it can be argued that there have been two conflicting social ideologies at work throughout history. These can be called individualism and collectivism.

Individualism promotes the notion that each individual is born with certain inalienable rights, which cannot be abrogated under any circumstances. From this perspective, the good of the individual is more important than the good of society taken as a whole.

Collectivism promotes the idea that the good of society, taken as a whole, is more important than the good of the individual people who make up the whole, and therefore a collection of individuals must be governed by certain laws, which, if necessary, can override individual rights.

These two perspectives seem to be mutually exclusive. Taken to their logical extremes they lead to different types of social organization. The absolute form of individualism results in social anarchy, where each person is free to pursue his or her own individual rights, without any restrictions imposed by law. The absolute form of collectivism, on the other hand, results in a totalitarian society, in which a small group of individuals sets the laws that all the others must abide by, even at the expense of their individual rights.

Neither of these systems can work under the corrupting influence of Ego. Corrupted by Ego, powerful individuals will abuse the rights of others and a totalitarian regime will abuse its total power by taking advantage of those under its control.

During the coming age of truth we will see a new type of

social system emerge, which embodies the best of both. I call this new social ideology "holism." This reflects the type of social ideology that exists in Nature.

For example, consider the society represented by the collection of cells within a healthy human body. In truth, each cell is created equal. Each cell contains exactly the same DNA as every other cell. Nevertheless, each cell finds its fulfillment in adopting a particular role in accordance with its environment. Some become brain cells, some become liver cells, some become muscle cells, etc.

By all playing their appointed roles, the cells thrive and prosper, without any sense of envy. Liver cells don't envy brain cells, and brain cells don't envy muscle cells—because each type of cell is devoid of Ego. Its true identity is determined by its DNA, which is the same in all, and not by its particular function.

Each individual cell, secure in its identity, finds complete fulfillment in performing its role in its own sphere of influence, and the spontaneous behavior of these individual cells serves to support the "good" of the body as a whole—without the need for any legislative laws. The physiology of the body operates according to natural laws, which manifest the will of God—not cell-made laws.

As individual conscious entities, brain cells might direct what the body is going to do at any particular time, but all of the other cells happily cooperate, because it is in their own best interest to do so and in the best interest of the body as a whole. This presents an example of social holism, where the principles of both individualism and collectivism are upheld simultaneously—and spontaneously.

No doubt, a social hierarchy may be implicit, but there is no class envy, or tendency for one level of the social hierarchy to abuse or take advantage of another—because every individual in the system is secure in its own identity and fulfilled by the role that it serves.

This type of system can also be translated into human society. The key is that the individuals involved be free from the corrupting influence of Ego, and secure in their true identity with the one universal Self—the same in all. In this case, a holistic social system could emerge that revolves around mutual service to one another and to all things in the universe taken as a whole.

In this ideal and natural type of social system, each individual would find fulfillment by serving the other individuals in its environment, in accordance with what it is best suited to do. The leaders of society would serve the people under their care with wise, selfless decisions and direction, and the people would serve each other and their leaders—with the intent of doing what is best in a given situation to foster the spiritual evolution of all.

By "all" I mean more than just the spiritual evolution of human beings on earth. I am talking about the spiritual evolution of everything—the plants, the animals, the minerals, the planets, the stars—the entire living universe.

In some cases, the spiritual evolution of the whole may involve self-sacrifice on the part of the individual, but under no circumstance is the true Self ever sacrificed—for it is immortal and completely uninfluenced by time, place, and circumstance.

The ancients thus held that there is no greater honor than to sacrifice one's individual life for the sake of the whole if the need ever arises. The key is that this be a "self-sacrifice"—a voluntary offering, inspired from within, and not something that is imposed from the outside.

This is a very high philosophy, which the human Ego finds

repugnant and difficult to understand. But once the Ego is eradicated and the true knowledge of the Self dawns in every human soul, it will be accepted as the natural philosophy. Only then can we resurrect a new more glorious form of human society based upon the ideology of holism, which simultaneously supports both the individualist and collectivist tendencies present in any society.

If our collective sacrifice, over the course of the next few years, serves to bring this new and holistic type of society about then I for one am willing to sign up and say "Let Thy will be done," for such a society will be in the best interest of each of us individually and in the best interest of the human race as a whole.

## The Emergence of Local Microcultures

However, I do not see this new holistic society as forming a centralized monoculture. That is not the way Nature works. The ecology of the earth is filled with local microcultures, each with its own unique charm and place in the overall biosphere.

Any attempt to eradicate these microcultures by replacing them with a monoculture, consisting of a single type of plant or a single type of animal is ultimately destructive.

The same thing holds true with respect to human society. Over the course of the last hundred years or so, the world has rapidly been moving toward the realization of a centralized monoculture, patterned after the "civilized" western way of life. This goal will never be realized because it is unnatural, destructive to the human soul, and designed with one thing in mind—control.

The human soul longs for individual expression on the basis

of universality. With the destruction of the Ego and the realization of the one eternal Self—the same in all—the worth of each individual soul will be secured. Human society will then flourish through the development of local microcultures, in which all individuals are free to express themselvee fully in accordance with the circumstances of time and place and the will of God—without having to conform to some arbitrary social standard.

As a result, each locale will develop its own unique cultural expression, its customs, dances, music, ritual observances, manners, patterns of dress and adornment, etc. in full accordance with the laws of nature in that area. There may be similarities between cultures of various regions, but there will be no attempt to force people to conform, or even any notion that they should conform—because all of that is a product of Ego and its insidious tendency to control its environment.

This will be possible because the engine that drives our current society will be gone. The lust for the accumulation of wealth and power will be absent—a situation that is hard to imagine. Moreover, the population will be greatly reduced.

For the most part food will be grown locally in an organic manner by taking advantage of the diversity of Nature and its self-replenishing ability. Rather than planting a single crop, the local farmers will plant a diversity of crops in the same plot. They will thereby create a local microculture, which is self-supporting and environmentally healthy. The emphasis will be upon taste and nutrition rather than quantity—yet the yields will be much larger than otherwise.

Trade also will be mostly local, and largely based upon a system of barter. Local currencies may evolve, but they will not be fiat currencies. Rather they will be tied to things of real value, and the system of centralized fractional reserve banking will be abolished.

In a holistic society, founded upon the principle of mutual service, there will be no hoarding of wealth. The highest use of wealth, once one's individual needs are met, will be to give it away freely to others. Just as Nature freely gives of its abundance, so also, human beings will share their abundance with each other. We will do this without any sense of regret, but with a profound sense of joy.

No doubt all of this may seem idealistic in the extreme, even utopian. But we are about to experience an extreme transformation in human consciousness, where none of the old rules apply. Our collective experience over the course of recorded history can tell us nothing about what is to come, because the human race will be operating on a completely different level of consciousness, knowledge, and motivation.

## The Rise of the Common Class

The old kingdoms, which emerged at the dawn of human civilization, were undoubtedly devoted to spiritual goals. But they cannot be used as models for what is to come. This is because they were rooted in the notion of elitism. They were designed to serve the elite classes of seer kings and seer priests.

This was in accordance with the nature of the cycle that is now coming to an end, a cycle that began in the age of Leo. The sign of Leo signifies royalty, specifically, as well as the nobility, and as a result, the current cycle was destined to mark the ascendancy of elites.

The coming cycle, on the other hand, will begin with the Age of Aquarius. The sign of Aquarius is the sign of the common class. As a result, the coming cycle will be destined to mark the ascendancy of the common man.

However, this will not represent a reduction to the lowest

common denominator. Every man and woman on earth will become like a king or queen—a sovereign embodiment of universal divine will. We will be benevolent, rather than tyrannical, kings and queens, whose lives will be devoted to nourishing and supporting those around them.

In the coming Age of Truth, the concept of private ownership will be a thing of the past, because each man and woman will literally experience the universe and everything in it as an expression of their own eternal Self. As possessors of all, as the kings and queens of the universe, we will be eternally satisfied with whatever happens to come our way—and if others are in need, we will gladly share with them whatever we have to spare.

Trying to apply current social principles, or even principles from the past, to the coming age simply will not work. Our current society and the future society can be compared to oil and water—they simply do not mix. For that reason, our current social system, rooted in ignorance, has to be destroyed before the new social system, rooted in knowledge, can arise.

Above all else, human consciousness must be transformed, and that is the real purpose of the coming global transformation. There is nothing at all that we can do to stop this transformation. It is part of our collective destiny. However, each of us individually is still endowed with free will. Each soul will be given the opportunity to choose how it will participate in the coming transformation. Which will you choose—to be a nourisher or destroyer?

Those who choose to be destroyers will be destroyed and banished from the face of the earth. Those who choose to be nourishers will be nourished, and they will inherit the earth. The decision is up to you. I have written this book in an attempt to make the options clear. I pray that each of us will make the right choice—both for our own sake and for that of the world.

# End Notes

[1] An ancient aphorism taken from the Rig Veda.

[2] Hesiod's *Work and Days,* lines 109-201.

[3] Hesiod's *Works and Days,* (lines 109-201), summary from Wikipedia article on the Ages of Man.

[4] *Hermetica,* Scott, p. 151-3

[5] Variously termed the Anthropos, Adam Kadmon, the Divine Man, Cosmos, or Lord Brahma.

[6] Hesiod's *Work and Days*, lines 109-201.

[7] Ovid's *Metamorphoses,* Book 1.89-150/

[8] In Sanskrit these were called *satya yuga* and *kali yuga* respectively.

[9] For example, See *Manu Smriti,* chapter 1.

[10] I don't believe this was an oversight or a mistake. The ancient Vedic texts were written by the enlightened seers for the enlightened seers, and in many cases things were left out. A number of these texts were written in an aphoristic style, where an entire complex subject was referenced by a short aphorism, consisting of a mere word or two. The enlightened seers believed that all knowledge could be accessed directly and intuitively within one's own consciousness, and that by merely indicating a subject using a word or two, those with enlightened vision would be able to apprehend the whole in great detail. To use a modern analogy, the brief description can be compared to the name of a file on a computer disc, which is to be opened and explored by those with enlightened vision.

[11] The central triangle is called *sarva siddhi pradha*—the bestower of all perfection.

[12] First Corinthians, 54-56.

[13] See *Manu Smriti*.

[14] An ancient aphorism taken from the Rig Veda.

[15] Genesis 2:17-18.

[16] For example, one might seek an instructor in the practice of Transcendental Meditation, as taught by the late Maharishi Mahesh Yogi. I can vouch that this technique is authentic. I myself have used it for decades.

[17] *Isha Upanishad,* 11

# About The Author

Robert E. Cox holds a master's degree in Vedic Studies from the Institute of Creative Intelligence in Switzerland. Living in monastic seclusion, he practiced long periods of meditation for nine years and received intuitive cognitions regarding the structure and dynamics of consciousness that have inspired his research in cosmology, physics, cycles of human history, and metallurgical alchemy. He is the author of *The Pillar of Celestial Fire*, *Creating the Soul Body*, and the forthcoming titles, *Elixir of Immortality*, and *Transcendental Mechanics*.

LaVergne, TN USA
14 November 2010

204821LV00007B/128/P